Mark Phillip Smith

Lake Tanganyika Cichlids

Everything About History, Setting Up an Aquarium, Health Concerns, and Spawning

Full-color Photographs
Illustrations by Michele Earle-Bridges

BARRON'S

2 CONTENTS

INTRODUCTION

The family Cichlidae encompasses a vast array of subtropical to tropical freshwater and brackish-water fish from both the Old and New World. It is also one of the fastest-growing families, with more than 20 new species described annually.

The cichlids of Lake Tanganyika have been among the most popular of freshwater aquarium fishes, particularly over the past 30 years. In the late 1970s they were a minor yet significantly popular group of fishes with cichlid enthusiasts the world over. When new areas of the lake began to be explored and new species brought out, there was a renaissance among cichlid hobbyists with new and spectacular species exported for the hobby. This trend continued unabated throughout the 1980s, 1990s and 2000s, making the cichlids of Lake Tanganyika firmly fixed in the tropical fish hobby and industry.

This Lamprologus meleagris, *with its compact, thickly set body, represents one of several dwarf Lamprologines inhabiting empty snail shells.*

Diversity of Cichlids

Of all the lakes on earth, Lake Tanganyika contains by far the most unique and diverse assemblage of freshwater fishes. From the 20 families of fishes represented in Lake Tanganyika, the one family that overshadows all others in diversity and numbers is the family Cichlidae. This family is represented throughout most of the African continent, in various river systems, and in all the other great lakes of Africa, yet the cichlids of Lake Tanganyika show a greater degree of adaptation and uniqueness of shape and habitat preference than those in any other lake or river system in Africa. In fact, most other categories of aquatic animal and plant life found in Lake Tanganyika show a similar degree of diversity.

The cichlids of Lake Tanganyika are unique in their polyphyletic origin, meaning that they come from several distinct ancestral lineages.

Lake Tanganyika's aquatic invertebrates have undergone a large-scale species radiation much like the cichlids have. Pictured is a Lake Tanganyika crab, Potamoautes platynotus, from Zambia.

In a 1986 review of the cichlids of Lake Tanganyika, Professor Max Poll defined 12 lineages or groups that are distinct from one another or that have a different ancestry. This is significant when you contrast the cichlid fauna of Lake Tanganyika to that of Lake Malawi, which has only three groups, one of which makes up more than 99 percent of that lake's cichlid fauna. Other African lakes such as Victoria, Kyoga, Edward, George, and Kivu also have one pre-

dominant lineage. In Lake Tanganyika, you can clearly see significantly distinct groups of species that are not closely related to one another, whereas in the other lakes, it is apparent that most of their species are closely related through their common ancestry.

Of the 12 distinct lineages, or "tribes," as Poll labeled them, eight are endemic to the lake, and the other four contain genera and species found outside the lake. Nevertheless, the vast majority of the species from the four nonendemic lineages, or tribes, are endemic to the lake proper. The tribes established by Poll are not without their inconsistencies, and recently some of them have been further divided and others united. Clearly, the final word on the precise classification of Lake Tanganyika's cichlids is not in yet and may not be for many years to come.

The History of Lake Tanganyika

How did such a diversity of species congregate in one lake? This question has intrigued ichthyologists for many years.

The formation of the lake began when the earth's crust ripped apart, creating a long tear in the earth's surface. Nearby rivers then began to pour into the great rift, eventually creating Lake

Perhaps the most cryptic group of noncichlids from the lake that possess a large number of species, both described and undescribed, are the Mastacembelid eels. Pictured is Ceacomastacembelus sp. "Micropectus Zambia" from shallow water. This undescribed species is the only member of the family that lacks pectoral fins.

Sandy shore at Chizanza, Zambia. Sandy areas of the lake act as barriers, preventing rock-bound cichlids from roaming and intermixing with nearby differing color variants of the same species.

Tanganyika. There is a consensus that, in the distant past, the lake existed as three smaller lakes. Over time, the level of the lakes rose and fell, connecting and then separating until the waters rose to connect all three into what is present-day Lake Tanganyika. It has been theorized that as various fishes invaded the ancient lakes from the surrounding rivers, they began to diversify and evolve into new species. As the levels of the lakes rose and joined, there was a mixing of genetic material—in other words, a redistribution of the fishes in each of the lakes. When

Rocky shoreline at Kala, Tanzania. The rising and falling of the lake level and the pounding of the surf over long periods of time have created isolated rocky zones. This has contributed to the isolation and formation of new species.

the water level receded to three lakes, a new amount of genetic material became isolated in each lake and the process of the creation of new species continued. The cycle of rising and receding may have repeated itself several times, thereby contributing to the formation of several new species before the lakes rejoined to form present-day Lake Tanganyika. After the three lakes merged into one lake for the last time, the water level continued to rise and submerge new stretches of dry land, which added additional biotopes for the cichlids to colonize. It has been theorized that during these processes, various rockbound species became segregated when, in the course of the effects of wave action, rocky areas broke up into isolated stretches separated from one another by substantial sandy zones. These separated populations of species continued to evolve into distinct color variants and new species; the result is what is seen today in Lake Tanganyika. These processes over time have resulted in approximately 220 species of cichlids presently known to inhabit Lake Tanganyika.

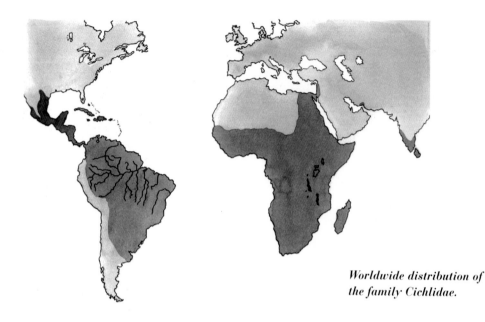

Worldwide distribution of the family Cichlidae.

General Facts

The lake, in East Africa, is bordered by four countries: the Congo (formerly Zaire) on the western side, Tanzania, on the eastern side, Burundi on the northeastern end, and Zambia at the southern end. It is around 420 miles (676 km) long and 40 miles (64 km) at its widest point, with a total shoreline length of approximately 1,000 miles (1,609 km). To give one a better grasp of the size of this lake, picture

that, if placed next to the state of California, it would stretch from San Francisco to Los Angeles. The lake is nearly 4,800 feet (1,463 m) deep at its deepest, and has deposits of sediments at the bottom that are more than 4 miles (6 km) thick in some areas! Oxygen penetrates down to approximately 650 to 700 feet (198–213 m), and beyond that, the remaining depths are anoxic and hold no permanent life. The water temperature is very stable and ranges from 76–82°F (26–27°C).

The chemistry of the water is constant throughout Lake Tanganyika. The pH ranges

One of the well known rock bound cichlids that have been influenced by the partitioning of sandy and rocky areas of the lake is this mouthbrooder, Eretmodus cyanostictus, from Zambia.

from 8.7 to 9.4, and the total carbonate hardness of the lake is 200 to 240 parts per million (ppm), or 12 to 14 degrees kH (German Hardness). This means that the lake water is quite alkaline and hard. One last picture of the physical nature of the lake is the transparency of the water. Visibility can be as much as 70 feet (21 m) in some places, especially around rocky islands where there is a lack of sediments from nearby rivers to cloud the water.

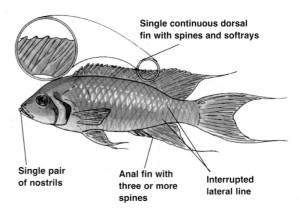

Single continuous dorsal fin with spines and softrays

Single pair of nostrils

Anal fin with three or more spines

Interrupted lateral line

External anatomy of a cichlid.

What Are Cichlids?

Cichlids are members of the order Perciformes that possess two fused lower pharyngeal bones (bones in the throat) in the shape of a triangle, which at a casual glance, appear to be a single bone.

Depending on the teeth present on this fused bone, one can make a good guess about what this fish feeds on. This triangular bone is not unique to cichlids. It is a feature shared by wrasses of the family Labridae, the surfperches of the family Embiotocidae, and the damselfishes of the family Pomacentridae. Additional features that distinguish cichlids are a single pair of nostrils, a toothless palate, an inter-

rupted lateral line, an anal fin with three or more spines, ctenoid or cycloid scales, and a single continuous dorsal fin composed of spines and soft rays.

Cichlids are categorized as secondary-division freshwater fishes. This means that the ancestors of today's cichlids were marine fish. At some

*Substrate spawning cichlids are no exception when it comes to displaying geographical variation and isolation due to alternating rocky and sandy zones along the shoreline. Pictured is an exceptionally attractive variant of **Julidochromis marlieri** from Kalambo, Tanzania.*

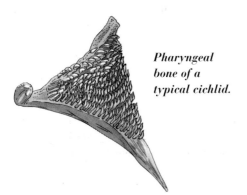

Pharyngeal bone of a typical cichlid.

The diversity of cichlid shapes found in Lake Tanganyika is truly astounding. This
Cyprichromis microlepidotus *from Kitumba, Congo epitomizes the slender, cylindrical open water species.*

time in the past, their ancestor invaded and successfully adapted to a freshwater environment. Cichlids are also egg-laying fishes that practice either mouthbrooding or substrate spawning as their mode of reproduction.

Additional anatomical structures that set cichlids apart from other kinds of fishes are as follows:
• subdivided cheek muscles allowing exact jaw movements
• a line showing the fusion point of the two halves of the lower pharyngeal bone
• a long deep furrow on the lateral face of the earbones

Cycloid (top) and ctenoid scales.

• the opening of the intestine always lying on the left side of the stomach and the first coil of the intestine always lying on the left side of the body

These internal features are not discernible while observing a living cichlid and can be determined only by dissection.

Cichlids are found throughout most subtropical and tropical areas of the world. In the Western Hemisphere, they range from southern Texas southward through Central and South America to the northern regions of Argentina and southern Uruguay. They are also present on the Caribbean islands of Cuba and Hispaniola. In the Old World, cichlids are found throughout sub-Saharan Africa, Israel, Syria, southern Iran at the Straits of Hormuz, Madagascar, southern India, and Sri Lanka. In these regions of the world, there are approximately 2,500 species, described and undescribed, with many more likely to be found in the near future. In fact, about 20 new species each year are formally described by scientists.

Neolamprologus brichardi, *pictured, is a male from Milima (Congo). It is perhaps the most recognizable cichlid from the lake, and comes in a variety of color variants around the lake.*

In regards to the noncichlid fishes of Lake Tanganyika, the species of the catfish genus Synodontis *show a large degree of variation in color pattern and species diversity. Pictured is a* Synodontis irsacae *from Zambia.*

SETTING UP YOUR AQUARIUM

Before acquiring Lake Tanganyika cichlids, the aquarist should be prepared to invest some time to understand the basic husbandry requirements that these fish require. That way, the hobbyist will be met with success the first time he or she sets up an aquarium.

Aquarium Size and Shape

The habitat preference of Lake Tanganyika cichlids is either bottom-oriented, or mid-water-oriented. The size and shape of the aquarium will be determined by the species you intend to maintain.

Lake Tanganyika cichlids are, by and large, naturally aggressive fishes. When aggressive species are placed in the restricted confines of an aquarium, you are likely to see an increase in aggressive behavior, particularly if the aquarium is too small.

If you decide to maintain bottom-oriented species, you should plan an aquarium with a large amount of bottom space and not as much height. Such an aquarium would provide more area to adequately decorate the bottom of the aquarium with rocks, which helps

Limnochromis auritus is an active digger that prefers sand in order to bring out its natural digging behavior.

bottom-oriented species feel secure. On the other hand, if you decide to maintain midwater-oriented species, an aquarium that is more tall than wide would be better, since many mid-water species prefer open spaces without the impediments of rocks.

The cichlids of Lake Tanganyika come in the widest possible size variation known for the family Cichlidae. They range in size from the diminutive shell-dwelling species such as *Neolamprologus multifasciatus* and *N. similis*, which attain a size of only $1^1/2$ inches (3.8 cm), to the giant *Boulengerochromis microlepis*, which can reach a length of 3 feet (94 cm)! If you plan on maintaining diminutive shell-dwelling species, a small aquarium of approximately 10 to 15 gallons (37.8–57 L) capacity will suffice. For a great majority of Lake Tanganyika cichlids, whose average size is approximately 3 to 6 inches (7.6–15 cm), a far larger aquarium of approximately 50 to 100 gallons (189–378.5 L) capacity would be prudent.

Proper mechanical, biological, and chemical filtration will help create favorable water conditions for Lake Tanganyika cichlids, such as this **Enantiopus** *sp. "Kilesa" from Kalumbie, Congo.*

Going to the other extreme, if you choose to maintain the world's largest cichlid species, *Boulengerochromis microlepis*, an aquarium of at least 250 gallons (946 L) capacity may work; a larger aquarium would most likely be needed to see this species grow to full size and perhaps even reproduce. Approximately $1/2$ inch (12 mm) of fish per gallon of aquarium water is a good rule of thumb to follow. Another factor that will determine the size of your aquarium is the number of fish you plan on maintaining. Think ahead and decide which species and how many of each you plan to maintain, then acquire the appropriate aquarium size and shape.

The Aquarium Stand

Aquariums are heavy for their size, and a sturdy, stable stand must be provided. Water weighs approximately 8 pounds per gallon, and added to the total weight of the water is the weight of the aquarium and the decorations in it. The stand needs to be not only sturdy

enough to handle all the weight, but also level, so that no one area of the aquarium or stand receives more weight and pressure than necessary. If a stand or aquarium is not completely level, placing a penny or two under the uneven portion of the stand works well.

Types of Filtration

Filtration is perhaps the most important aspect of proper aquarium fish husbandry that needs to be understood before you can successfully maintain any fish in the confines of a captive environment. To safely maintain fishes in an aquarium, their water must be filtered (processed). There are three types of aquarium filtration, and a combination of all three is ideal.

Biological Filtration

The first and most important type of filtration is biological, a type that is crucial to keeping fishes in a closed environment—without it, it is impossible to maintain fishes in an aquarium. Any organic material, such as fish waste, uneaten food, decaying plant matter, or dead, rotting fish is mineralized by heterotrophic bacteria, with the result that ammonia is produced. Ammonia is exceedingly toxic to fishes. Additional bacteria further oxidize the ammonia into nitrites, and still other bacteria convert the nitrites to nitrates. This is the nitrification process, or biological filtration in its simplest form.

When you first install a biological filter, it takes approximately four to six weeks to grow enough bacteria to efficiently process your fishes' excrement, uneaten food, and decaying plant matter. A common method to begin the four- to six-week maturation process is to use "test fish." These can be any species of tropi-

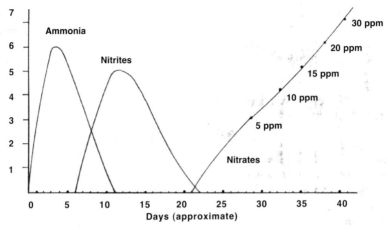

The cycling process of biological filtration.

cal fish that is extremely hardy and can with-stand high concentrations of ammonia and nitrites. Some of the more commonly used, inexpensive, and hardy test fish are the Paradise Gourami—*Macropodus opercularis*—and the Blue Gourami—*Trichogaster tricopterus*. These labyrinth fishes will normally survive the spike of ammonia and nitrite during the cycling process. Such test fish should be maintained and fed daily in the newly set-up aquarium until it has cycled. It is advisable not to perform any water changes during this period. After the aquarium has cycled, perform a 50 percent water change, remove the test fish, and add your prized Tan-ganyika cichlids.

The best way to follow the cycling process of your biological filter is to invest in test kits for ammonia, nitrite, and nitrate. Test your newly set-up aquarium daily and monitor any change that takes place; you can also have your water tested at any reputable tropical fish dealer. Over the course of the first few days, you will see a spike in the amount of ammonia in the water. As the ammonia recedes to negligible levels, the nitrites will spike, then slowly recede to negligi-ble levels as you begin to get your first nitrate readings. When nitrites are no longer present, the aquarium has matured and the cycle is complete.

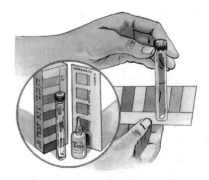

Regular maintenance should include testing for ammonia, nitrate, nitrite, pH, and hardness.

If you need to adjust the alkalinity and hardness of your Tanganyika cichlid aquarium, any number of high-quality Tanganyika cichlid buffering salts can be used.

Biological filtration also produces hydrogen ions that lower the pH in the aquarium, making the water more acidic. The easiest way to combat this is to maintain a regular schedule of water changes (see page 23). Frequent water changes will help maintain a stable environment for your Tanganyika cichlids. In addition to preventing the water from becoming acidic, water changes will help to lower the nitrate levels. The overall well-being of your aquarium residents depends on regularly changing water.

Chemical Filtration

The second form of filtration is chemical, which may consist of carbon or various pelleted resins used to absorb harmful chemicals from the water. This type of filtration is useful if your local municipal water supply is contaminated with a variety of chemicals. Chemical filtration is also useful for removing medications from the water after the medicines have effected a cure.

Mechanical Filtration

The third form of filtration is mechanical. This form of filtration simply removes visible particulate matter as water passes through a filtering medium so that the water remains free of unsightly sediments.

Whatever form of filtration you decide to use, it should biologically filter the water in a consistent and adequate manner. It should also mechanically filter the water to remove visible organic material, and it should have the capacity to chemically filter the water to remove any harmful chemicals that may be present. You will need to make sure that the filter does not become clogged with organic material, thereby producing excessive amounts of nitrates. Regularly servicing your filter and performing water changes on a regular basis will help to keep the nitrates at low levels, as well as prevent the water from becoming acidic.

Maintaining appropriate water chemistry to the liking of Lake Tanganyika cichlids, like this Xenotilapia flavipinnis *from Magara, Burundi, is recommended for their long term health.*

It is important for you to use a water conditioner to neutralize the chlorine or chloramine that local municipal water companies regularly add to the water supply.

Aquarium Water Chemistry

Because the cichlids of Lake Tanganyika are found in waters of high pH and alkalinity, it would be wise to attempt to match your aquarium water to that of the lake. It may be impossible to precisely duplicate the water chemistry of Lake Tanganyika in your aquarium, but you can condition your aquarium water in the right direction, and in doing so, achieve a modest facsimile. The pH in the lake ranges from about 8.7 to 9.4 with a total mineral hardness of 12 to 14 kH, or German hardness (approximately 200 to 240 ppm of carbonate hardness), making the lake water very alkaline with a high mineral concentration. Most municipal water comes out of the faucet with a pH of approximately 7.4 to 7.6 and a total mineral hardness that may vary substantially, depending on your local water source. It is recommended that you invest in test kits that measure for pH and water hardness, or at least have your water tested at a local retail tropical fish establishment so that you will be able to determine whether your water needs buffering to increase the pH and kH. If your aquarium needs to be buffered to increase the pH and kH, a number of products are on the market that you can use.

If you live in an area where your tap water has a relatively high pH and kH, nothing more needs to be done, other than to add a water conditioner to remove any chlorine, chloramine, heavy metals, and other contaminants.

Remember to add water conditioner to all new water put into your aquarium.

Heater and Thermometer

Tanganyika cichlids come from water with a temperature of approximately 76–82°F (26–27°C); therefore, a heater is usually necessary. Aquariums up to 100 gallons (378.5 L) will probably need only one appropriately sized heater, whereas aquariums much larger should have two heaters, one at each end of the aquarium, for greater temperature stability. You will need to read the suggested heater size on the box of the heater before making a

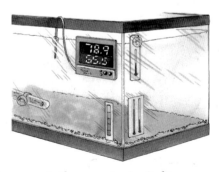

An accurate thermometer is vital to establish the correct water temperature.

Subdued lighting is recommended for many Lake Tanganyika cichlids, such as this Altolamprologus compressiceps.

The habitat preference for this Julidochromis transcriptus from Katoto, Zambia is bottom oriented, among the caves and crevises created by rocks randomly piled up.

purchase; it will give you a guideline for the size and wattage your aquarium needs. A general guide to follow is about 3 watts per gallon. For example, a 50-gallon (189 L) aquarium would need a 150-watt heater. The heater should be mounted in the aquarium only after it is full of water. Remember to allow about half an hour for the heater's internal thermostat to adjust itself to the temperature of the water before turning on your heater. At this point, install an accurate thermometer.

Lighting

Proper lighting enables you to observe your Tanganyika cichlids more clearly. Most fluorescent bulbs used to illuminate aquariums seem to rob Tanganyika cichlids of some of their colors, especially if the artificial light source is too strong. Natural sunlight is ideal but not always possible to achieve. Placing an aquarium next to a window works well, but you will need to be sure that the sunlight does not heat the aquarium water.

Fluorescent bulbs are most often the lighting of choice. If you decide to use fluorescent bulbs, choose those designed to give off white or daylight lighting. Also, cichlids need to sleep much as we do, so keep the lights on only during the day, and turn them off at night.

Decorations

Determining what kind of decorations to use will depend on what species of Tanganyika cichlid you plan to keep. Tanganyika cichlids have two habitat preferences. These are midwater-oriented and bottom-oriented. If you plan to maintain bottom-oriented species, provide a thin layer of fine sand for the sand-dwelling species or several smooth rocks piled up to form caves and passageways for the rock-bound species. Jagged lava rocks should be avoided since they may injure your Tanganyika cichlids if they accidentally scrape against the sharp edges. If very large rocks are used, a small piece of Styrofoam can be placed underneath the sections of the rock that will

Altolamprologus calvus prefers to have rocks or caves piled up in such a manner as to create narrow crevices, the preferred hiding place for this laterally compressed species.

be in contact with the glass. This will protect the bottom pane.

For the midwater-oriented Tanganyika cichlids, only a few smooth rocks are recommended, with most of the bottom open with a thin layer of sand. The few smooth rocks will provide a degree of refuge, help to demarcate territories, and provide a greater sense of security.

Gravel/Sand

Most of us want to have some gravel or sand in our aquariums. It is not only pleasing to the eye, but hides the bottom of the tank from view. However, having too much gravel or sand will invite all kinds of bacteria to form anaerobic conditions in the deeper recesses of the gravel/sand bed, so it is advisable not to have too much. If you maintain an undergravel filter,

a standard 2 inches (5 cm) of gravel depth will suffice. If you do not maintain an undergravel filter, a fine layer of no more than $1/2$ inch (1 cm) of silica sand will do.

Decorations, such as sharp rocks, should be kept to a minimum for open water Lake Tanganyika cichlids, such as this Cyprichromis sp. *"Jumbo Leptosoma" from Karilani Island, Tanzania.*

HOW–TO: LEARNING ABOUT

There are many types of filters on the market. Most do a fair job of maintaining adequate water quality, but some are more efficient than others. Learn about the most popular types before you decide on the best one for your cichlids.

The trickle filter. Trickle filters supply great biological filtration, particularly for heavily stocked, large aquariums. Be sure to carefully monitor the buildup of organic material within the filter, and remove it regularly during routine filter maintenance.

Undergravel Filter

Undergravel filters have long been very popular for both salt- and freshwater aquariums. A plate is placed under the gravel. Water is drawn down through the gravel by a submersible water pump or air-driven stone, through the plate, and circulated back into the aquarium via a tube at the back end of the plate. Bacteria accumulate in the gravel bed so that the gravel bed becomes one big biological filter. These filters provide good biological filtration at first, but eventually they become so saturated with organic material that they become nitrate-producing factories. They perform an aver-age job at providing mechanical filtration and provide absolutely no chemical filtration. Organic material eventually translates into the production of nitrates through the nitrification process, so it is important to remove as much organic material as possible to keep nitrates to a minimum. With undergravel filters this is nearly impossible. Over time—approximately one year—this type of filter will collect more organic material than you will be able to remove, resulting in the production of high levels of nitrates, far higher than regular water changes will be able to control.

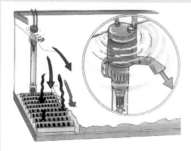

The undergravel filter provides good biological filtration, but over time it will produce excess amounts of nitrates, particularly if not gravel-vacuumed frequently.

Trickle Filter

The trickle filter is an excellent biological filter, particularly if you wish to filter large aquariums. Oxygen saturation is achieved in this filter as the drops of water trickle through the ball-like filter medium. The pre-filter acts as the mechanical portion of this filter, and a small chamber next to the filter medium holds chemical filtering material. Over time, the plastic balls and other internal parts of the filter gather more and more organic material, which, in turn, produces large quantities of nitrates. If the plastic balls are periodically flushed of their organic buildup, and/or a small portion periodically replaced with new plastic balls, excessive amounts of nitrates should not be a recurring problem. Also, as part of regularly maintaining any filter, you will need to examine the inside of the filter to make sure it is functioning optimally and remove any

FILTERS

buildup of organic material from the walls and floor of the filter. It is also important to remove the buildup of organic material that collects inside the intake and outtake tubes.

Canister Filter

Canister filters provide the three types of filtration already mentioned. However, they require a lot of servicing to keep the collection of organic material inside the canister to a minimum. They can be difficult and messy to clean, something that most of us use as an excuse to put off regular maintenance. It is important to keep the pre-filter clean so as not to impede water flow through the canister filter.

Box Filter

Box filters are capable of providing all three types of biological filtration, but must be serviced frequently to keep organic material from building up to the point of producing large amounts of nitrates as the product of biologically filtered water. Some hobbyists have modified box filters to contain only dime-sized lava rocks in the lower half of the chamber while having a thick piece of sponge on the top half of the chamber. The lava rocks provide the surface space for nitrifying bacteria to colonize and thus provide for biological filtration, and the sponge acts as a pre-filter, preventing organic material from collecting on the lava rocks. This type of filter seems to function best when the sponge is rinsed thoroughly once a week. It is ideal for aquariums no larger than 30 or 40 gallons (113.5–151 L).

Sponge Filter

Sponge filters are excellent for small aquariums and for raising juvenile cichlids; their

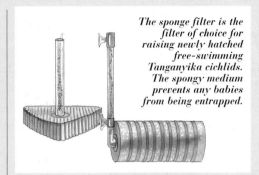

The sponge filter is the filter of choice for raising newly hatched free-swimming Tanganyika cichlids. The spongy medium prevents any babies from being entrapped.

surface area is too small to entrap juvenile cichlids. Eventually, the sponge will break down and need to be replaced, so the process of reestablishing a biologically mature filter must start again. You can avoid this by starting up another sponge filter two months before replacing the old one.

Biological Wheel Filter

One filter on the market provides all three types of filtration and that can be quickly and easily cleaned of its organic buildup without compromising its biological filtering capability. This filter is the Bio-Wheel, which has a biological component, a corrugated wheel situated in the pathway of the water return. As water is returned to the aquarium, it pours over the corrugated wheel, and the bacteria on the wheel convert the ammonia to nitrite and then into nitrate. This arrangement also allows for a great deal of oxygen to saturate the water, something needed not only by fish, but also by the nitrifying bacteria. The back chamber of the filter provides for mechanical and chemical filtration in the form of a filter pad that can easily be replaced before becoming clogged with organic material.

MAINTAINING THE AQUARIUM

Once the Lake Tanganyika cichlid aquarium has been set up, it must be regularly maintained. Doing so will assure the cichlids' long-term health.

Water Changes

Changing water on a regular basis is the single-most important task of aquarium fish keeping. Several factors will determine when, how much, and how often you should change your aquarium water. The number of Tanganyika cichlids you are maintaining, the amount of food given at each feeding, and how many times a day your Tanganyika cichlids are fed will all determine your water-changing routines. Approximately 25 percent of the volume of the aquarium's water should be changed weekly or 33 percent every two weeks in an aquarium that is sparsely populated ($\frac{1}{2}$ inch [12.7 mm] of fish per gallon). If you crowd your Tanganyika cichlids (1 to 2 inches [2.5–5 cm] of fish per gallon), then 40 percent water changes weekly, or

Regular, frequent water changes should be a standard function of keeping Lake Tanganyika cichlids, such as these Tropheus duboisi from Maswa, Tanzania.

60 percent water changes every two weeks should be standard procedure. These are rough guidelines, and you may need to change more or less water, depending on the number of fish and the quantity of food given.

Test Kits

Invest in high-quality test kits. Once your biological filter has cycled, you will primarily be testing for nitrate levels, which will give you an indication of when a water change is required. Ideally, your Tanganyika cichlids should not be exposed to nitrate concentrations beyond 20 ppm for extended lengths of time. Tanganyika cichlids can survive high nitrate readings for a while, but maintaining them in water with nitrates substantially higher than 20 ppm over long periods of time is asking for trouble. Tanganyika cichlids kept in water with high nitrates over long periods of time will become weakened and unable to resist bacterial or parasitic infections.

The natural diet of this **Aulonocara dewindti** *from Zambia consists of sand-dwelling invertebrates in the wild. Make every attempt to duplicate the diet of your Lake Tanganyika cichlids with similar food items.*

Siphoning

A siphon hose will be an invaluable piece of equipment for performing water changes. Water from the bottom of the aquarium should be siphoned out; if you have gravel or sand in your aquarium, a modified siphon hose with a wide mouth at the intake end is recommended. This widened end should be placed into the gravel or sand so that the siphoning action will lift the detritus out while leaving the substrate behind.

Any new water being placed into the aquarium should first be thoroughly conditioned with a water conditioner from your local tropical fish dealer. The temperature of the new water should be the same as that of the aquarium water, and never cooler.

Aeration

The aquarium water should be saturated with oxygen at all times. Not only do your Tanganyika cichlids need oxygen to survive, but so do the bacteria in your biological filter. A clear sign that not enough oxygen is present in the water can be seen when your Tanganyika cichlids stay near the top of the aquarium with their mouths nearly touching the surface, gasping for what little oxygen is left. Making sure that enough oxygen is present in the water can be accomplished by the use of an air-stone/air-pump combination, or an outside power filter trickling water back into the tank, agitating the surface.

Diet

In their natural habitat, the various species of Tanganyika cichlids live on a wide variety of foods: algae, fishes, scales of other cichlids, snails, microinvertebrates, plants, crabs, shrimps, and plankton. It is interesting to note that in their natural habitat, Tanganyika cichlids will consume other kinds of foods for which they were not specifically designed. For example, *Petrochromis* and *Tropheus*, considered herbivorous, will not hesitate to eat baby fishes or the eggs of substrate-spawning cichlids.

Therefore, some flexibility in the Tanganyika cichlids' diet is permissible, but the primary food source they were specifically designed to consume should be simulated as closely as possible.

Parasites and Bacterial Infections

A multitude of parasites and bacterial infections occur sporadically in tropical fishes, but only a few seem to be recurrent problems with Tanganyika cichlids. The easiest thing to do to minimize the risk of your Tanganyika cichlids having a particular ailment—parasite or bacterial infection—is to practice good husbandry

Ich, or Ichthyophthirius multifilis, *is the most commonly encountered parasite in the aquarium hobby. Fortunately, is it easy to cure with the proper over-the-counter medicines. Pictured is a male* Ophthalmotilapia ventralis *from Sumbu, Zambia.*

skills. These efforts will assure a healthy environment for your fish that will in turn result in healthy, vigorous cichlids. It is only when the needs of your Tanganyika cichlids are not being met that they begin to become stressed. Their immune systems weaken considerably when they become stressed, and they will not be able to fight off parasitic or bacterial infections. The result will often be that your Tanganyika cichlids develop debilitating ailments that will need medicinal treatment if they are to survive. If your Tanganyika cichlids come down with parasites or a bacterial infection, the following information may be helpful.

Ichthyophthirius

Ich, or *Ichthyophthirius multifilis*, is probably the most commonly encountered parasite to attack fish in the aquarium. It seems to rear its head when fish are stressed because of a sudden drop in temperature. This parasite may not manifest itself for several days, and may attach itself only inside the gills of the host fish. If ich confines itself to the gills, it will be nearly impossible to detect at first; your fish may die for no apparent reason. At other times, you will see tiny white dots sprinkled over the fish's body, something like the color and size of salt grains. In whichever area of the body ich manifests itself, the affected fish will probably glance off objects in an effort to scratch itself.

Fortunately, ich is one of the easiest parasitic infections to treat. Malachite green is the most readily available medicine one can use to treat it. Ich has a three-day life cycle, so the medicine should be in the water for at least three days; four to five is better. It is important to remove any carbon from your filter before using medicine, because the carbon will absorb the medicine, rendering it ineffective. A slight rise in water temperature will help to speed up the life cycle of the ich and help the medicine effect a cure a little sooner. A 25 to 50 percent water change after the completion of treatment is advisable along with the addition of fresh carbon to absorb any residual medication that may still be present in your aquarium.

Bloat

Another ailment that commonly affects Tanganyika cichlids, particularly those species that tend to be herbivorous, is bloat. Bloat is caused when the fish's intestinal tract becomes infected and inflamed. The inflammation is caused by improper diet—for example, high-protein foods for herbivorous species—too much of the same kind of food, or poor water quality. This condition, unless treated immediately, may result in the death of the fish within a

Good husbandry practices help prevent bloat (top), eye infection (middle), and hole-in-the-head disease (bottom).

few days. If treated immediately upon signs of first symptoms (loss of appetite, a noticeable distension of the body region, and an increased respiratory rate), a cure may be possible, but is not always guaranteed. The medication metronidazole is often used at 1/8 teaspoon per 20 gallons

(76 L) of water once a day for three to five days. After the completion of treatment, perform a 50 percent water change and add carbon to the filter to absorb any residual medication.

Eye Infections

Several large-eyed Tanganyika cichlid species may be prone to developing eye infections. This usually begins when the cichlid scratches its eye against a sharp object in the aquarium. The infection takes hold invariably when the water quality is poor and the injured cichlid has been stressed for some length of time. Medications with silver nitrate as the active ingredient are specially designed to treat eye infections. This medication must be applied to the infected eye twice a day. Unfortunately, this means that the fish needing treatment must be removed from the water. This is a difficult condition to treat, and a cure is not always achieved.

Hole-in-the-Head

Hole-in-the-head, or lateral line disease, is caused by an infestation of flagellate protozoans attacking the sensory pores of a fish's head, as well as its lateral line. Cichlids with this infection show pitting on the sides of the face and on the lateral line system on the sides of the body. Some species seem to be more prone to developing this malady than others; you can keep its occurrence to a minimum by maintaining scrupulous aquarium conditions and making sure that your cichlids are being fed a well-balanced diet. Metronidazole may stop hole-in-

This large eyed Lake Tanganyika cichlid, Haplotaxodon microlepis, may be prone to eye infections if there are too many sharp objects in the aquarium.

Newly acquired Lake Tanganyika cichlids, such as this **Paracyprichromis brieni** *from Kapemba, Congo, should be quarantined before being placed together with your collection of fishes.*

the-head from spreading, but once the damage has been done, scarring will remain on the face and lateral line.

Quarantine Aquarium

A method often employed by hobbyists and professionals is the use of a quarantine aquarium to house newly acquired fish. Tanganyika cichlids may be stressed, and may carry a bacterial infection or internal or external parasites in the dealer's holding tank. If they were to be placed directly into your main aquarium with your other Tanganyika cichlids, the newly introduced cichlid might infect the other aquarium inhabitants. A quarantine aquarium need be only 10 gallons (37.8 L). It should have an established biological filter and no chemical filtration. A heater and thermometer is needed to maintain a constant temperature of 80°F (26.7°C). There should be no gravel in the aquarium, which would make it more difficult to keep the aquarium clean during treatment.

Always examine the fish you intend to purchase, looking for clamped fins, heavy breathing, or white salt-like spots on the body, as these are signs of an unhealthy fish. Pictured is a perfectly healthy **Lamprologus ocellatus** *from Nkamba Bay, Zambia.*

The aquarium should not be lighted overhead, and enough shelter should be placed inside so that the quarantined fish will feel safe and secure. If the fish is stressed because it cannot find a place to hide, it may not respond quickly to treatment.

With a quarantine aquarium set up and running properly, any newly acquired fish should be placed into it for approximately one month. During this time, care for the quarantined fish in the same manner as you would any other aquarium fish. If the fish has a bacterial infection or parasites, it will become apparent within a month's time. At the first sign of such ailments, the quarantined fish should be treated with the proper medication until it is completely cured; only then should it be placed into the main aquarium.

SPAWNING LAKE TANGANYIKA CICHLIDS

Those hobbyists interested in reproducing Lake Tanganyika cichlids should start out with species that are easiest to spawn.

Laying the Groundwork

One rewarding facet of maintaining Tanganyika cichlids is spawning them. The first step is to decide which species of Tanganyika cichlid you wish to work with, taking into consideration your aquarium limitations and available funds. A reputable tropical fish dealer or specialty cichlid club are two sources that may offer a wide variety of Tanganyika cichlids for sale. Some hobbyists choose to start out with wild adults, whereas others begin with captive-raised juveniles. You need to be careful with the latter method, since in all likelihood, the juveniles you purchase may have originated from the same parents.

Make sure to offer your Lake Tanganyika cichlids, such as the Telmatochromis *sp. "Temporalis Shell," foods with natural color enhancers, such as live baby brine shrimp.*

What ends up happening is that brother and sister are bred to each other, their offspring in turn are spawned back to each other, and so on. The result of such indiscriminate captive spawnings are fish that look very little like their wild-caught kin.

Avoiding Inbreeding

You can do two things to minimize this often repeated practice of inbreeding. The first is to work with wild-caught specimens. If you are not able to afford or find wild-caught specimens, the second option is to obtain high-quality captive-bred stock. High-quality captive-bred stock are specimens with the color and body shape closely matching that of wild-caught specimens. Carefully compare the species you wish to obtain with photos depicting either wild-caught specimens, or captive-bred specimens, that have maintained their wild appearance.

This juvenile **Neolamprologus marunguensis** *does not yet possess the filamentous tipped doral, caudal, and anal fins of the adults.*

When obtaining captive-bred juveniles, make an effort to buy one or two specimens from different sources so that the likelihood of breeding brother to sister will be greatly diminished. Every effort to propagate wild-caught or high-quality captive-bred stock is crucial.

Habitats for Spawning

Tanganyika cichlids are egg-laying fish that practice substrate-spawning or mouthbrooding as a means of reproduction. Species that practice substrate-spawning lay their eggs on a surface such as a stone, sandy pit, or empty snail shell. Species that practice mouthbrooding incubate their eggs in their mouths. Usually, the female is given all the honors, but in some species both male and female participate in the oral incubation of the eggs.

An aquarium supplied with rocks piled up to form caves and crevices is ideal for most of the substrate-spawning species. An inverted flowerpot with a small hole punched in the side works well, as do small ceramic caves specially designed to provide refuge for small fish. For the shell dwellers, several empty marine snail shells placed over a shallow sandy substrate will do.

Mouthbrooding Tanganyika cichlids have two general habitat preferences. Your aquarium should reflect these variations, depending on the species you want to work with. Species of the genera *Tropheus, Petrochromis, Eretmodus, Spathodus,* and *Tanganicodus* inhabit the rocky regions of the lake, and will undoubtedly need a lot of shelter in the form of rocks. For many mouthbrooding species of the genera *Ectodus, Bathybates, Hemibates, Benthochromis, Trematocara, Paracyprichromis, Cyprichromis,* and most *Xenotilapia,* an open, spacious aquarium with few rocks is preferable. The males of many mouthbrooding species can be quite aggressive toward unresponsive or brooding females, so provide a small amount of shelter in the form of rocks, an inverted flowerpot, or PVC piping to allow any overly harassed female an opportunity to hide and avoid the male's territorial or sexually aggressive tendencies.

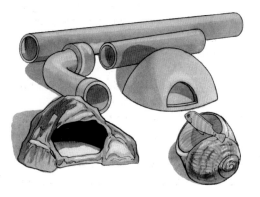

Various natural and artificial spawning structures.

This wild caught **Julidochromis transcriptus** *from Gombi, Zambia shows a rich and desireable color pattern. The progeny of such Tanganyika cichlids should be cultivated whenever possible.*

Difficult-to-Breed Species

Some of the naturally aggressive species may prove difficult to breed in captivity. Males of certain hyperaggressive species display astounding levels of aggression toward any subdominant male or female of their own kind, invariably resulting in the death of the subdominant individual. This can be a real challenge if you have your heart set on maintaining and spawning a particularly aggressive species. Fortunately, there are some things you can do to minimize the aggression and encourage peaceful spawning:

1. Crowd your aquarium with only the species you wish to work with and remove all possible hiding places. This will have the effect of spreading out the aggression of the dominant male, as well as robbing it of establishing a territory, so that it does not focus on any one fish. If it is faced with too many of its own kind to chase after, the dominant male might become more mellow with this arrangement, but close attention must be given to maintaining good water quality. Stocking an aquarium to its limit is risky and will result in greater quantities of waste being produced. The buildup of waste products must be dealt with by increased water changing and frequently examining, cleaning, or replacing the disposable filter pad of your filter to make sure it is functioning capably.

2. Divide the aquarium in two with a single male on one side and a single female on the other side. An egg crate, which is a light-diffusing ventilated panel, works well. It can be found in the lighting department of your local hardware store. Any other sturdy, nontoxic structure that permits free water flow and allows the pair to see each other through the divider is acceptable. When the pair is ready to

The habitat for spawning Bathybates species should be a large, open aquarium with no decorations, and only a shallow layer of fine sand. Pictured is a juvenile Bathybates minor.

This difficult to spawn species, Benthochromis tricoti, requires a largel aquarium with one or two males and several females. No other fish should be present. After spawning, provide live brine shrimp to the spawning aquarium daily, as the developing juveniles will feed upon the shrimp while still in the mother's mouth for several weeks.

spawn, they will do so next to the divider. If the divider has sufficient ventilation, the male's sperm will easily pass through the divider and fertilize the female's eggs. The female can then care for her clutch of eggs without being molested by the male. Or, you can create a hole in the divider, just large enough for the smaller female to pass through, but small enough to prevent the male from passing through. This way, once the female is ready, she can pass

through the hole in the divider into the male's territory and successfully spawn. If the male becomes too rough on the female, she will then retreat back through the hole in the divider to the safety of her side of the aquarium.

Dither Fishes

"Dither fishes" are defined as any species of fish that are incidental to your primary aquarium residents. Often they are non-cichlid species that are active open-water dwellers, such as rainbow fishes of the family Melanotaeniidae,

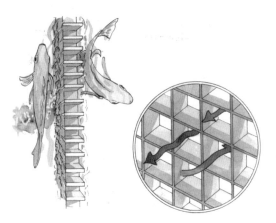

An aquarium divider is a practical way to spawn highly aggressive Tanganyika cichlids. The holes in the divider permit the male to fertilize the female's eggs, while at the same time preventing the male from overly harassing or even killing the female.

Providing dither fish for your Lake Tanganyika cichlids, *such as this* Neolamprologus *sp. "Ventralis Kasanga" female, will aid in strengthening an existing pair bond.*

or catfish of the genus *Synodontis*. The use of dither fishes often has the effect of helping to create or sustain a pair bond with many substrate-spawning Tanganyika cichlids. Parental Tanganyika cichlids perceive the dither fish as a threat to their offspring, which in turn stimulates them to be more vigilant in guarding their offspring against the "threat" of the dither fish. Dither fishes should be hardy, active, and peaceful fishes that are capable of withstanding the potential aggression of your Tanganyika cichlids.

Raising Juvenile Tanganyika Cichlids

Baby Brine Shrimp

One of the best first foods for juvenile Tanganyika cichlids is live baby brine shrimp, *Artemia nauplii*. They are easy to hatch out, and make an excellent first food. Brine shrimp eggs can be obtained through your local tropical fish dealer, or from specialty companies that advertise in aquarium-related magazines. Be careful not to overfeed juvenile Tanganyika cichlids. They seem to have a propensity for gorging themselves to the point of death if given too much food. It is better to give them several

Be careful not to overfeed your juvenile Lake Tanganyika cichlids, such as this juvenile Telmatochromis dhonti *from Kavalla, Congo.*

small feedings per day rather than one or two giant feedings. If there is any uneaten food or waste on the bottom of the aquarium, siphon it out, replacing the old water with properly conditioned fresh tap water. As the fish grow and consume more food, it will be necessary to get the young fish accustomed to larger, more frequent water changes of 25 to 50 percent weekly.

This 40-day old juvenile Bathybates fasciatus *has reached the size of 2 inches (5 cm). It can now be offered foods larger than live baby brine shrimp.*

The most rewarding way to obtain offspring from parental Tanganyika cichlids is to let them do what comes naturally. One of the most satisfying experiences you'll have in breeding Tanganyika cichlids will be observing and studying the behavior of parents and offspring. There may come a time when you want to separate the babies from their parents and raise them on their own, particularly when the presence of the juveniles begins to crowd the aquarium, or when other aquarium residents begin to consume the juveniles.

If you maintain a single breeding pair of substrate-spawning Tanganyika cichlids in a modest-sized aquarium, you may not have to remove the juveniles until they reach a length of 3/4 inch (19 mm) or whenever the parents chase them from the spawning site. At this size, the juveniles can easily be netted from the aquarium. Or you can remove the juveniles just after they have become free-swimming.

Siphoning

The easiest way to remove free-swimming juveniles is to siphon them out while they are asleep. Wait until late evening after all the lights have been turned out for several hours, then turn on the aquarium lights and, before the juveniles have a chance to wake up, siphon them into a nearby tank. This way, the juveniles never leave the water and do not have to endure any changes in water composition or temperature during the move. Afterward, gently pour the juveniles

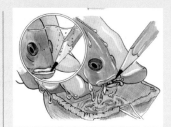

With wet hands, gently hold the brooding female in one hand and, with a pencil in the other, carefully pry open its mouth over the parents' aquarium with a net in place. After the juveniles have been released from the female's mouth, the net full of babies can be immediately transferred to a grow-out aquarium.

into a separate grow-out aquarium that has been filled with water from the parents' aquarium. Make sure that the temperature in the grow-out aquarium is the same as that of the parents' aquarium.

Counting Off the Days after Spawning

When breeding mouth-brooding Tanganyika cichlids, make note of the day that your mouthbrooders have spawned and count off approximately 18 to 21 days, the length of time it usually takes for freshly fertilized Tanganyika cichlid eggs to develop into free-swimming young. Exceptions to this time period are species of the genera *Tropheus*, *Petrochromis*, *Bathybates*,

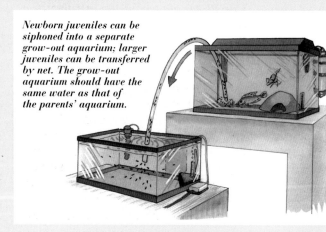

Newborn juveniles can be siphoned into a separate grow-out aquarium; larger juveniles can be transferred by net. The grow-out aquarium should have the same water as that of the parents' aquarium.

Hemibates, and *Cyphotilapia,* which take around 35 days for their eggs to develop, and the species of the genera *Perissodus, Plecodus, Reganochromis, Benthochromis,* and *Haplotaxodon,* which take between 11 and 14 days. The best course of action is to continue to observe your mouthbrooding Tanganyika cichlid and take note when it is on the verge of releasing its babies to forage. If too many other cichlids that may pose a threat to the hatchlings are present, the brooding parent may hold off releasing them for several days. If only the parents are present, leaving the brooding parent alone to release its young is the best course to follow. It can be very rewarding to see firsthand your parental Tanganyika cichlids releasing their offspring.

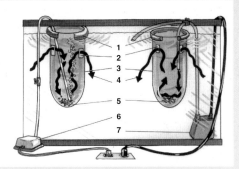

Two types of artificial incubators for mouthbrooding cichlid eggs.

1. *flotation device*
2. *vents*
3. *inverted plastic soda bottle*
4. *water current*
5. *embryo eggs*
6. *air pump*
7. *water pump*

Releasing the Brood

You may want to save as many juveniles as possible, since mouthbrooding Tanganyika cichlids generally do not produce as many young as substrate-spawning Tanganyika cichlids. When it comes time for the parent (usually the female) to release its brood, you can choose to strip it of its free-swimming young. This is where counting the 18 to 21 days from the first day of its spawning becomes important. Stripping the juveniles from the parent's mouth should take place on the last day of the countdown from the day of the initial spawning. The most trouble-free way to catch the parent is while it is asleep. Again, wait until the lights have been out for several hours, then turn on the lights and immediately catch the parent with a net before it wakes up. This way, the parent will not panic. Gently grab the parent with one hand, previously wetted, and with a sharpened pencil in the other hand, carefully pry open its mouth, gently shaking it in and out of the water while holding it over the net. The

juveniles should begin to trickle out into the net. Continue this process until all the juveniles have been expelled from the parent's mouth. Afterward, return the parent to the breeding aquarium or place it in another aquarium to recuperate if needed. Quickly place the juveniles into the grow-out aquarium that you've prepared beforehand with water from the parents' aquarium.

Artificial Incubation

If you are working with a mouthbrooding Tanganyika cichlid that will not hold its clutch of eggs to full term, you may want to artificially incubate the embryos. A typical incubator for mouthbrooding cichlid eggs consists of a small container set up inside an aquarium that, by means of aeration or gentle current, keeps the eggs in constant motion, permitting their proper development into free-swimming juveniles. The container should be clear so that you can monitor the development of the eggs and embryos.

REPRESENTATIVE SELECTION OF LAKE TANGANYIKA CICHLIDS

Lake Tanganyika cichlids come in the most amazing variety of shapes, from large-mouthed robust species to dwarf shell-dwelling species. They also display a huge range in size, from 1 inch (2.5 cm) to 3 feet (90 m).

Name: *Altolamprologus calvus*
To 6 inches (15 cm)
Distribution: Southwest area between Kapampa, Congo, and Cape Chaitika, Zambia. Inhabits rocky areas between 10 and 135 feet (3–41 m) deep.
Husbandry: >50 gallons (189 L). A mild-mannered species. Provide rock crevices to stake out as a territory and future spawning site.
Diet: Aquatic invertebrates and small fish. Offer foods high in protein, such as live guppies, live aquatic brown worms, and chopped live earthworms.
Breeding: Substrate spawner. Female will select a small cave or recess in a rock too small

above: **Altolamprologus calvus** *male from Chaitika, Zambia.*
left: Close-up of the unique lip structure in **Gnathochromis permaxillaris.**

for the male to enter. The female remains with the eggs/larvae until they become free-swimming at 11 days. Offer juveniles live baby brine shrimp.

Name: *Altolamprologus compressiceps*
To 6 inches (15 cm)
Distribution: Widespread in shallow water over rocky/sandy habitats.
Husbandry: Relatively peaceful cichlid, but will not hesitate to consume small fish. Provide rock crevices to stake out as a territory and future spawning site.
Diet: Aquatic invertebrates and small fish. Offer foods high in protein, such as live guppies, live aquatic brown worms, and chopped live earthworms.
Breeding: Substrate spawner. Female will select a small cave or recess in a rock too small for the male to enter. The female remains with the

Altolamprologus compressiceps *from Cape Chaitika, Zambia.*

Asprotilapia leptura *male from Cameron Bay, Zambia.*

eggs/larvae until they become free-swimming at 11 days. Offer juveniles live baby brine shrimp.

Name: *Altolamprologus fasciatus*
To 6 inches (15 cm)
Distribution: Widespread except for the extreme northern part. Inhabits rocky areas less than 40 feet (12 m) deep.
Husbandry: >30 gallons (113.5 L). A peaceful species, not to be maintained with overly aggressive lamprologines. Provide rocks piled up to form caves and passageways.
Diet: Shrimp and juvenile crabs. Offer high-protein foods such as frozen shrimp, live feeder guppies, aquatic brown worms, and mysis shrimp.

Adult male Altolamprologus fasciatus *are typically 4 times the size of females.*

Breeding: Substrate spawner. Will spawn in empty snail shells or other narrow structures. Juveniles are very slow-growing. Offer juveniles live baby brine shrimp.

Name: *Asprotilapia leptura*
To 5 inches (13 cm)
Distribution: Widespread to a depth of 40 feet (12 m) over a mix of rocks and sand.
Husbandry: >50 gallons (189 L). Gregarious; kept in groups of at least eight. Provide a few smooth stones and a shallow layer of silica sand.
Diet: Algae and microinvertebrates on rocks. Will consume most prepared aquarium foods. Include spirulina-based foods.
Breeding: Biparental mouthbrooder. Female first holds the eggs for approximately 11 days, then the male broods them for an additional 11 days. Offer juveniles live baby brine shrimp.

Name: *Aulonocranus dewindtii*
To 6 inches (15 cm)
Distribution: Widespread in very shallow water over sandy rocky areas.
Husbandry: >50 gallons (189 L). Maintain in small groups of five to six. Only one male should be present; any other subdominant males will

Aulonocara dewindtii *male from Kigoma, Tanzania.*

Bathybates fasciatus *male from Zambia.*

not be tolerated unless the aquarium is more than 100 gallons (378.5 L) capacity.

Diet: Sand-dwelling invertebrates. Will eat most prepared aquarium foods. Include daphnia, mysis shrimp, and live baby brine shrimp.

Breeding: Maternal mouthbrooder. Male may build a small, sandy pit as a spawning site. Eggs develop in 21 days. Offer juveniles live baby brine shrimp.

Name: *Bathybates fasciatus*
To 13 inches (33 cm)

Distribution: Widespread from the surface down to 500 feet (152 m).

Husbandry: Minimum 150 gallons (568 L). Adaptable cichlid in spite of its highly specialized morphology and diet in the wild. Very mild mannered. Aquarium should be devoid of any rockscaping.

Diet: Feeds primarily on the lake sardines. In captivity, readily adapts to prepared dried and frozen foods, silversides, and feeder guppies.

Breeding: Maternal mouthbrooder, producing large 7 mm eggs. Raise several together in large aquarium (>150 gallons [568 L]). Spawning should commence at 15 to 18 months old.

Name: *Bathybates ferox*
To 15 inches (38 cm)

Distribution: Widespread from the surface down to 150 feet (45 m).

Husbandry: >150 gallons (568 L). Adaptable cichlid in spite of its highly specialized morphology and diet in the wild. Very mild mannered. Aquarium should be devoid of any rockscaping.

Diet: Feeds primarily on the lake sardines. In captivity, readily adapts to prepared dried and frozen foods, silversides, and feeder guppies.

Breeding: Maternal mouthbrooder, producing large 7 mm eggs. Raise several together in large aquarium (>150 gallons [568 L]). Spawning should commence at 15 to 18 months old.

Bathybates ferox *is one of the more shallow water dwelling species of Bathybates.*

Bathybates minor is the smallest species of the genus Bathybates.

Name: *Bathybates minor*
To 8 inches (20 cm)
   Distribution: Widespread from the surface down to 500 feet (152 m).
   Husbandry: >75 gallons (283 L). Adaptable cichlid in spite of its highly specialized morphology and diet in the wild. Very mild mannered. Aquarium should be devoid of any rockscaping.
   Diet: Feeds on the lake sardines. In captivity, readily adapts to prepared dried and frozen foods, silversides, and feeder guppies.
   Breeding: Maternal mouthbrooder, producing large 7 mm eggs. Raise several together in large

Juvenile Benthochromis melanoides are virtually identical to juvenile B. tricoti, and juveniles of both species school together.

Benthochromis tricoti is known to practice prolonged mouthbrooding care of its young, often for over 2 months.

aquarium (>75 gallons [283 L]). Spawning should commence at 9 to 15 months old.

Name: *Benthochromis melanoides*
To 8 inches (20 cm)
   Distribution: Widespread in open water near the coast from 65 feet (20 m) to 300 feet (90 m) deep.
   Husbandry: Provide a very large, deep, and dimly lighted aquarium (>200 gallons [757 L]), silica sand and many open spaces, and only a couple of large, flat, smooth stones. Best maintained in a colony to themselves.
   Diet: Zooplankton. Offer high-protein aquarium foods such as live baby brine shrimp, mosquito larvae, and live aquatic brown worms.
   Breeding: Maternal mouthbrooder. Will not spawn if intimidated by other tankmates. Has yet to reproduce in captivity.

Name: *Benthochromis tricoti*
To 8 inches (20 cm)
   Distribution: Widespread in open water near the coast from 65 feet (20 m) to 300 feet (90 m) deep.

Boulengerochromis microlepis *may be the largest species of cichlid known.*

Husbandry: Provide a very large, deep, and dimly lighted aquarium (>200 gallons [757 L]), silica sand, and many open spaces, and only a couple of large, flat, smooth stones. Best maintained in a colony to themselves.

Diet: Zooplankton. Offer high-protein aquarium foods such as live baby brine shrimp, mosquito larvae, and live aquatic brown worms.

Breeding: Maternal mouthbrooder. Will not spawn if intimidated by other tankmates. Eggs hatch and embryos become free-swimming after 16 days at a length of $^2/_5$ of an inch (10 mm). The female will continue brooding the juveniles until they reach a length of $1^1/_4$ inches (3.2 cm). During this extended brooding period, provide copious quantities of live baby brine shrimp, in the spawning aquarium, for the juveniles to consume while still in the female's mouth.

Name: *Boulengerochromis microlepis*
To 36 inches (91 cm)
Distribution: Throughout the lake in sandy/rocky areas.
Husbandry: >300 gallons (1,135 L). Moderately aggressive; small groups can be raised together. Best raised in a community setup to keep any aggression to a minimum. Needs lots of space and frequent, large water changes to maintain optimum health.

Diet: Piscivore. Offer a variety of aquarium foods high in protein.

Breeding: In the wild, parents do not eat after spawning has commenced. Both parents protect their brood until they die of starvation. Offer juveniles live baby brine shrimp.

Name: *Callochromis melanostigma*
To 6 inches (15 cm)
Distribution: Found in the extreme northern end, primarily in Burundi. Lives at depths of less than 20 feet (6 m) over sandy areas near scattered rocks.
Husbandry: >75 gallons (283 L). Maintain at least eight together. Only one male per 75 gallons, as dominant males are intolerant of each other.
Diet: Sand-dwelling invertebrates. Offer commercially prepared aquarium food. Supplement diet with small live or frozen daphnia, mysis shrimp, and brine shrimp.
Breeding: Maternal mouthbrooder. Dominant male will construct a sandy pit and display to all

Callochromis melanostigma *was among the first sand-dwelling cichlids to be exported from the lake. Pictured is a male from Burundi.*

Callochromis pleurospilus *male from* **Kigoma, Tanzania.**

females. After spawning, the brooding female(s) should be isolated from the male. Eggs develop in 21 days. Offer juveniles live baby brine shrimp.

Name: *Callochromis pleurospilus*
To 4 inches (10 cm)
Distribution: Widespread. Inhabits shallow sandy areas.
Husbandry: >50 gallons (189 L). Maintained in groups of at least eight. Provide a thin layer of silica sand along with a couple of smooth stones to demarcate territories.
Diet: Sand-dwelling invertebrates. Offer commercially prepared aquarium food. Supplement diet with small live or frozen daphnia, mysis shrimp, and brine shrimp.
Breeding: Maternal mouthbrooder. Dominant male will construct a sandy pit and display to all females. After spawning, the brooding

female(s) can be left with the dominant male. Eggs develop in 16 days. Offer juveniles live baby brine shrimp.

Name: *Callochromis stappersii*
To 4 inches (10 cm)
Distribution: Central Tanzanian coastline. Inhabits shallow sandy areas.
Husbandry: >50 gallons (189 L). Maintained in groups of at least eight. Provide a thin layer of silica sand along with a couple of smooth stones to demarcate territories.
Diet: Sand-dwelling invertebrates. Offer commercially prepared aquarium food. Supplement diet with small live or frozen daphnia, mysis shrimp, and brine shrimp.
Breeding: Maternal mouthbrooder. Dominant male will construct a sandy pit and display to all females. After spawning, the brooding female(s) can be left with the dominant male. Eggs develop in 16 days. Offer juveniles live baby brine shrimp.

Name: *Chalinochromis brichardi*
To 6¹/₂ inches (16.5 cm)
Distribution: Congo (formerly Zaire), Burundi, and Zambian coastline in rocky areas.
Husbandry: >75 gallons (283 L). Raise several together in a mixed community setting with other substrate-spawning Tanganyika cichlids. Aquarium should be heavily rockscaped.

Callochromis stappersii *has the most limited distribution of any* **Callochromis** *species, being found only along the central Tanzanian coastline.*

Chalinochromis brichardi *juveniles begin life with two horizontal black stripes on the body, changing to spots and eventually to no pattern, as seen in this male from Magara, Burundi.*

Chalinochromis sp. *"Bifrenatus" maintains its juvenile color pattern of two horizontal stripes throughout its adult life. Pictured is a male from Kigoma, Tanzania.*

Diet: Microinvertebrates. Offer a variety of aquarium foods high in protein. Supplement the diet with live brown worms and mysis shrimp.

Breeding: Substrate spawner. Requires a cave to deposit eggs and brood young. Pair may become extremely aggressive. Offer juveniles live baby brine shrimp.

Name: *Chalinochromis* sp. "Bifrenatus"
To 6½ inches (16.5 cm)
Distribution: Central Tanzanian coastline in rocky areas.
Husbandry: >75 gallons (283 L). Raise several together in a mixed community setting with other substrate-spawning Tanganyika cichlids. Aquarium should be heavily rockscaped.
Diet: Microinvertebrates. Offer a variety of aquarium foods high in protein. Supplement the diet with live brown worms and mysis shrimp.
Breeding: Substrate spawner. Requires a cave to deposit eggs and brood young. Pair may become extremely aggressive. Offer juveniles live baby brine shrimp.

Name: *Chalinochromis* sp. "Ndobnoi"
To 6 inches (15 cm)
Distribution: Central Tanzanian coastline in rocky areas.
Husbandry: >75 gallons (283 L). Raise several together in a mixed community setting with other substrate-spawning Tanganyika cichlids. Aquarium should be heavily rockscaped.
Diet: Microinvertebrates. Offer a variety of aquarium foods high in protein. Supplement the diet with live brown worms and mysis shrimp.

Chalinochromis sp. *"Ndobhoi" adult from Bulu Point, Tanzania.*

Breeding: Substrate spawner. Requires a cave to deposit eggs and brood young. Pair may become extremely aggressive. Offer juveniles live baby brine shrimp.

Name: *Chalinochromis popelini*
To 6 inches (15 cm)
Distribution: Central western coast from Cap Tembwe to Moba, Congo, in shallow rocky areas.
Husbandry: >75 gallons (283 L). Raise several together in a mixed community setting with other substrate-spawning Tanganyika cichlids. Aquarium should be heavily rockscaped.
Diet: Microinvertebrates. Offer a variety of aquarium foods high in protein. Supplement the diet with live brown worms and mysis shrimp.
Breeding: Substrate spawner. Requires a cave to deposit eggs and brood young. Pair may become extremely aggressive. Offer juveniles live baby brine shrimp.

Name: *Ctenochromis benthicola*
To 7 inches (18 cm)
Distribution: Widespread from 10 to 150 feet deep (3 m to 45 m) deep. Very secretive rock dweller, seldom leaving the hidden recesses of caves.
Husbandry: >100 gallons (378.5 L) minimum. Aquarium should have many rocks to provide refuge and overall security.

The true **Chalinochromis popelini** *has three horizontal stripes and a crescent-shaped caudal fin. Pictured is a male from Cap Tembwe, Congo.*

Diet: Small fish and aquatic invertibrates. Offer all types of aquarium foods. Supplement diet with shrimp, live feeder guppies, and live aquatic brown worms.
Breeding: Has not yet reproduced in captivity. Likely a maternal mouthbrooder.

Name: *Ctenochromis horei*
To 7 inches (18 cm)
Distribution: Widespread in shallow water in close proximity to aquatic plants.
Husbandry: >100 gallons (378.5 L) minimum. Highly aggressive cichlid toward its own kind. Aquarium should have many rocks to provide refuge for less dominant individuals.
Diet: Omnivorous. Offer all types of aquarium foods. Supplement diet with spirulina-based foods.
Breeding: Maternal mouthbrooder. Difficult cichlid to reproduce because of the male's

Female xanthic mutation of **Ctenochromis benthicola.** *Recent scientific surveys found it to be very common in water less than 15 feet (4.5 m) deep.*

Ctenochromis horei is an extremely aggressive species in captivity and requires very clean water.

Cyathopharynx furcifer male from Isanga, Zambia.

aggressiveness. If there are enough hiding places, or if the divider method is used, spawning may be successful. Eggs develop in 12 to 14 days. Offer juveniles live baby brine shrimp.

Name: *Cyathopharynx foae*
To 9 inches (23 cm)

Distribution: Widespread in shallow water where large rocks and sand intermingle.

Husbandry: >100 gallons (378.5 L). Provide plenty of silica sand for the dominant male to construct a nest.

Diet: Zooplankton and phytoplankton. Offer commercially prepared aquarium foods. Supple-

Cyathopharynx foae male from Kigoma, Tanzania.

ment diet with small live or frozen daphnia, mysis shrimp, and mosquito larvae.

Breeding: Maternal mouthbrooder. Dominant male will coax any receptive female into its nest to spawn. After spawning, the brooding female(s) should be isolated from the male. Eggs develop in 21 days. Offer juveniles live baby brine shrimp.

Name: *Cyathopharynx furcifer*
To 9 inches (23 cm)

Distribution: Southeast Tanzanian and Zambian shoreline in shallow water where large rocks and sand intermingle.

Husbandry: >100 gallons (378.5 L). Provide plenty of silica sand for the dominant male to construct a nest. Very sensitive to poor water quality.

Diet: Zooplankton and phytoplankton. Offer commercially prepared aquarium foods. Supplement diet with small live or frozen daphnia, mysis shrimp, and mosquito larvae.

Breeding: Maternal mouthbrooder. Dominant male will coax any receptive female into its nest to spawn. After spawning, the brooding female(s) should be isolated from the male. Eggs develop in 21 days. Offer juveniles live baby brine shrimp.

The true **Cyphotilapia frontosa**, *according to the original description in 1906, corresponds to the seven-striped specimen pictured here from Kigoma, Tanzania.*

Name: *Cyphotilapia frontosa*
To 16 inches (40.6 cm)

Distribution: Kigoma, Tanzania, over rocky areas from 35 to 350 feet (10.5–105 m) deep.

Cyphotilapia gibberosa *was recently described to include the 6-striped individuals in the southern half of the lake.*

Husbandry: >200 gallons (757 L). Best maintained in groups of at least eight. Do not maintain with any cichlid small enough to fit into its mouth. Provide plenty of rocks piled up to form large spaces and passageways.

Diet: Small fish, and macroinvertebrates. Offer a variety of aquarium foods such as fresh-frozen shrimp and pellets.

Breeding: Maternal mouthbrooder. One male will spawn with several females. Eggs are large and take approximately 35 days to develop into free-swimming juveniles. Offer juveniles live baby brine shrimp.

Name: *Cyphotilapia gibberosa*
To 16 inches (40.6 cm)

Distribution: Southern half of the lake from Kilewa Bay, Congo, and Myako, Tanzania, southward over rocky areas from 35 to 350 feet (10.5–105 m) deep.

Husbandry: >200 gallons (757 L). Best maintained in groups of at least eight. Do not maintain with any cichlid small enough to fit into its mouth. Provide plenty of rocks piled up to form large spaces and passageways.

Diet: Small fish, and macroinvertebrates. Offer a variety of aquarium foods such as fresh-frozen shrimp and pellets.

Breeding: Maternal mouthbrooder. One male will spawn with several females. Eggs are large

Cyprichromis sp. "Jumbo Leptosoma" male from Kitumba, Congo.

Cyprichromis microlepidotus male from Rutunga, Burundi.

and take approximately 35 days to develop into free-swimming juveniles. Offer juveniles live baby brine shrimp.

Name: *Cyprichromis* sp. "Jumbo Leptosoma"
To 5 inches (13 cm)
Distribution: Southern coastline in open water near boulders.
Husbandry: >75 gallons (283 L). Maintain at least eight together in a tall aquarium with plenty of open space.
Diet: Zooplankton. Will eat most prepared aquarium foods small enough to fit into its mouth. Include live baby brine shrimp.
Breeding: Maternal mouthbrooder. Dominant male will stake out a territory and proceed to coax any nearby female to spawn in midwater. Brooding females hold for approximately 21 days. Offer juveniles live baby brine shrimp.

Name: *Cyprichromis microlepidotus*
To 5 inches (13 cm)
Distribution: Northern coastline in open water near boulders at a depth of 35 to 130 feet (10.5–39 m).
Husbandry: >75 gallons (283 L). Maintain at least eight together in a tall aquarium with plenty of open space.

Diet: Zooplankton. Will eat most prepared aquarium foods small enough to fit into its mouth. Include live baby brine shrimp.
Breeding: Maternal mouthbrooder. Dominant male will stake out a territory and proceed to coax any nearby female to spawn in midwater. Brooding females hold for approximately 21 days. Offer juveniles live baby brine shrimp.

Name: *Ectodus* sp. "North"
To 5¹/₂ inches (14 cm)
Distribution: Northern half of the lake. Inhabits shallow sandy areas.
Husbandry: >50 gallons (189 L). Provide one male and several females. Aquarium should consist of fine silica sand and few smooth stones, if any.
Diet: Sand-dwelling invertebrates. Offer a variety of commercially prepared aquarium foods. Supplement the diet with live brine shrimp, aquatic brown worms, and daphnia.
Breeding: Maternal mouthbrooder. Dominant male constructs a pit in the sand and will coax any nearby female to spawn. Eggs develop in 18 days. Offer juveniles live baby brine shrimp.

Ectodus sp. "North" from Burundi. Notice the subtle blue hue in the dorsal fin in this sexually active male.

Eretmodus cyanostictus is remarkably gobylike in its shape and lifestyle.

Name: *Enantiopus* sp. "Kilesa"
To 6 inches (15 cm)

Distribution: Central western shores of Congo, between Kavalla and Kalemie. Inhabits shallow sandy areas.

Husbandry: >75 gallons (283 L). Provide one male and several females. Aquarium should consist of fine silica sand approximately 2 inches (5 cm) deep.

Diet: Sand-dwelling invertebrates. Offer a variety of commercially prepared aquarium foods. Supplement the diet with live brine shrimp, aquatic brown worms, and daphnia.

Breeding: Maternal mouthbrooder. Dominant male constructs a large pit in the sand with small piles of sand around the perimeter. Receptive females are coaxed into the nest to spawn. Eggs develop in 21 days. Offer juveniles live baby brine shrimp.

Name: *Eretmodus cyanostictus*
To 3 1/2 inches (9 cm)

Distribution: Southern half of the lake in the upper 10 feet (3 m) of the surf zone over small stones.

Husbandry: >40 gallons (151 L) and heavily strewn with smooth rocks. Maintain in groups of at least six. Provide moderate current with highly oxygenated water.

Diet: Algae growing on rocks. Offer foods high in spirulina and algae.

Breeding: Biparental mouthbrooder. Female incubates the eggs for approximately 11 days at first; then the embryos are transferred to the male, who incubates them for an additional 11 days. Offer juveniles live baby brine shrimp and finely crushed spirulina flakes.

Enantiopus sp. "Kilesa" from Kavalla, Congo, is one of the most striking sand-dwellers known.

Name: *Gnathochromis permaxillaris*
To 8 inches (20 cm)
   Distribution: Throughout the lake over muddy/sandy areas from 100 to 330 feet (30–99 m) deep.
   Husbandry: >150 gallons (568 L). Provide PVC piping with one end buried in silica sand, as a cave for dwelling and spawning in.
   Diet: Zooplankton. Offer a wide variety of aquarium foods.
   Breeding: Delayed biparental mouthbrooder. Eggs are initially laid in a deep cave. After a few days, larvae are brooded by the female and then by the male. Use a long piece of PVC piping, capped at one end. The other end should be buried in silica sand and the pair allowed to dig and find the long, deep cave. Spawning should occur within the piping. Offer juveniles live baby brine shrimp.

Gnathochromis permaxillaris is best known for its greatly enlarged upper lip.

Name: *Greenwoodochromis christyi*
To 7 inches (18 cm)
   Distribution: Throughout the southern part of the lake in sandy/rocky areas deeper than 80 feet (24 m).
   Husbandry: >100 gallons (378.5 L). Provide rocks piled up to form caves and passageways. Maintain with its own kind or with other similarly aggressive species.
   Diet: Small fishes. Offer high-protein foods such as shelled fresh shrimp, live feeder guppies, and frozen or freeze-dried ocean plankton.
   Breeding: Biparental mouthbrooder. Female begins brooding process for 8 to 11 days, then male finishes incubating period. Offer juveniles live baby brine shrimp.

Greenwoodochromis christyi male from Chituta Bay, Zambia.

Name: *Haplotaxodon microlepis*
To 11 inches (28 cm)
   Distribution: Throughout the lake over rocky areas no deeper than 70 feet (21 m).

Haplotaxodon microlepis is a large species, reaching about 11 inches (27.5 cm), and sports four vertical bars underneath the dorsal fin.

Husbandry: Relatively peaceful cichlid, provided aquarium is at least 100 gallons (378.5 L). Provide a few large smooth rocks scattered among silica sand.

Diet: Small fish and zooplankton. Possibly feeds on the eggs and young of mouthbrooding Tanganyika cichlids. Offer prepared aquarium foods, and supplement the diet with small live feeder guppies and fresh-frozen shelled shrimp.

Breeding: Maternal mouthbrooder. Yet to reproduce in captivity.

Name: *Haplotaxodon trifasciatus*
To 5¹/₂ inches (14 cm)
Distribution: Zambia to southern Congo coastline over rocky areas no deeper than 70 feet (21 m).
Husbandry: Relatively peaceful cichlid, provided aquarium is at least 50 gallons (189 L). Provide a few large smooth rocks scattered among silica sand.

Hemibates stenosoma has rarely been imported into the hobby.

Haplotaxodon trifasciatus is a small species, reaching about 5¹/₂ inches (13 cm), and only sports three vertical bars underneath the dorsal fin.

Diet: Small fish and zooplankton. Possibly feeds on the eggs and young of mouthbrooding Tanganyika cichlids. Offer aquarium foods, and supplement the diet with small live feeder guppies and fresh-frozen shelled shrimp.

Breeding: Maternal mouthbrooder. Eggs brooded by the female for 16–18 days. Offer baby brine shrimp to babies.

Name: *Hemibates stenosoma*
To 11 inches (28 cm)
Distribution: Widespread in water deeper than 300 feet (90 m) during the day, but in shallow water at night.
Husbandry: >100 gallons (378.5 L). Adaptable cichlid in spite of its highly specialized morphology and diet in the wild. Very mild mannered. Aquarium should be devoid of any rockscaping.
Diet: Feeds primarily on the lake sardines. In captivity, readily adapts to prepared dried and frozen foods, silversides, and feeder guppies.
Breeding: Maternal mouthbrooder, producing large 7 mm eggs. Raise several together in large aquarium (>100 gallons [378.5 L]). Spawning should commence at 12 to 15 months old.

Name: *Hemibates* sp. "Stenosoma Zambia"
To 13 inches (33 cm)
Distribution: Zambian waters deeper than 300 feet (90 m) during the day, but in shallow water at night.
Husbandry: >100 gallons (378.5 L). Likely to be adaptable in spite of its highly specialized morphology and diet in the wild.

An exciting new find is this undescribed Hemibates sp. "Stenosoma Zambia." Its larger size, differing color pattern, and smaller eye size in relation to the size of the head clearly sets it apart as a new species.

Diet: Feeds primarily on the lake sardines.

Breeding: Maternal mouthbrooder, producing large 7 mm eggs. Has yet to be maintained in captivity.

Name: *Julidochromis dickfeldi*
To 4 inches (10 cm)

Distribution: From Kapampa, Congo, to Ndole, Zambia. Inhabits the rocky areas to a depth of around 65 feet (20 m).

Husbandry: >30 gallons (113.5 L). Provide plenty of rocks to form passageways and caves.

Diet: Microinvertebrates. Offer a variety of aquarium foods high in protein. Supplement the diet with live brown worms and mysis shrimp.

Breeding: Substrate spawner. Prefers to lay its eggs and brood its young in caves. Free-swimming juveniles hug the rocks surrounding the spawning site for the first few weeks. Offer juveniles live baby brine shrimp.

Name: *Julidochromis marlieri*
To 6 inches (15 cm)

Distribution: Northern third and the southern third of the lake. Inhabits the rocky areas to a depth of around 100 feet (30 m).

Julidochromis dickfeldi has more blue coloration on its fins than any other Julidochromis species.

Husbandry: >30 gallons (113.5 L). Provide plenty of rocks to form passageways and caves.

Diet: Microinvertebrates. Offer a variety of aquarium foods high in protein. Supplement the diet with live brown worms and mysis shrimp.

Breeding: Substrate spawner. Prefers to lay its eggs and brood its young in caves. Free-swimming juveniles hug the rocks surrounding the spawning site for the first few weeks. Offer juveniles live baby brine shrimp.

Julidochromis marlieri was one of the first cichlids to be exported from the lake. Pictured is a male from Rutunga, Burundi.

This **Julidochromis ornatus** *from Uvira, Congo, is one of the prettiest species of dwarf* **Julidochromis.**

Julidochromis regani *from Sumbu, Zambia.*

Name: *Julidochromis ornatus*
To 3¹/₂ inches (9 cm)
Distribution: Uvira, Congo, and in Zambia, in rocky areas between 15 and 130 feet (4.5–39 m) deep.
Husbandry: Easily maintained as a pair in aquariums as small as 15 gallons (57 L). Main-tain in >50 gallons (189 L) in a community set-ting. Provide rock work in the form of caves and passageways.
Diet: Microinvertebrates. Offer a variety of aquarium foods. Supplement the diet with live aquatic brown worms, frozen bloodworms, and brine shrimp.
Breeding: Substrate spawner. Spawning will occur within the rocks. Offer juveniles live baby brine shrimp.

Name: *Julidochromis regani*
To 6 inches (15 cm)
Distribution: Occurs in scattered populations throughout in rocky/sandy areas no deeper than 35 feet (11 m).
Husbandry: >50 gallons (189 L). Provide many rocks forming passageways and caves.
Diet: Microinvertebrates. Offer a variety of aquarium foods high in protein. Supplement the diet with live brown worms and mysis shrimp.
Breeding: Substrate spawner. Prefers to lay its eggs and brood its young in caves. Free-swimming juveniles hug the rocks surrounding the spawning site for the first few weeks. Offer juveniles live baby brine shrimp.

Name: *Julidochromis* sp. "Regani Kipili"
To 5 inches (13 cm)
Distribution: Kilipi to Kerenge Island, Tanza-nia. Inhabits the rocky areas to a depth of around 100 feet (30 m).
Husbandry: >50 gallons (189 L). Provide many rocks forming passageways and caves.

Julidochromis *sp. "Regani Kipili" has become a very popular species since it was first collected several years ago. Pictured is a male from Kipili, Tanzania.*

Diet: Microinvertebrates. Offer a variety of aquarium foods high in protein. Supplement the diet with live brown worms and mysis shrimp.

Breeding: Substrate spawner. Prefers to lay its eggs and brood its young in caves. Free-swimming juveniles hug the rocks surrounding the spawning site for the first few weeks. Offer juveniles live baby brine shrimp.

Name: *Julidochromis transcriptus*
To 3¹/₂ inches (8.9 cm)

Distribution: Uvira and Kapampa on the western shoreline in Congo, at Samazi, Tanzania, at Gombe, Zambia, in rocky areas between 15 and 80 feet (4.5–24 m) deep.

Husbandry: Easily maintained as a pair in aquariums as small as 15 gallons (57 L). Maintain in >50 gallons (189 L) in a community setting. Provide rock work in the form of caves and passageways.

Diet: Microinvertebrates. Offer a variety of aquarium foods. Supplement the diet with live aquatic brown worms, frozen bloodworms, and brine shrimp.

Breeding: Substrate spawner. Spawning will occur within the rocks. Offer juveniles live baby brine shrimp.

Name: *Lamprologus brevis*
To 2 inches (5 cm)

Distribution: Widespread in sandy areas with empty snail shells.

Husbandry: Ideal cichlid for those with limited aquarium space. Can easily be maintained in aquariums as small as 10 gallons (38 L). One empty aquatic snail shell per individual should be provided along with a thin layer of silica sand.

Julidochromis transcriptus *female from Gombe, Zambia.*

Diet: Sand-dwelling invertebrates and plankton. Offer a variety of aquarium foods. Supplement diet with live baby brine shrimp and aquatic brown worms.

Breeding: Substrate spawner. Spawning takes place in female's shell. Male and female form a monogamous bond and provide protection at the perimeter of the territory. Offer juveniles live baby brine shrimp.

Lamprologus brevis *was one of the first shell-dwelling cichlids to be exported from the lake.*

Name: *Lamprologus caudopunctatus*
To 2¹/₂ inches (6 cm)

Distribution: Southern shoreline among rocky/sandy areas from 15 to 70 feet (4.6–21 m) deep.

Husbandry: >25 gallons (95 L). Gregarious species that should be kept in groups of at least eight. Provide caves and rocks piled up to form passageways.

Diet: Zooplankton. Offer a variety of aquarium foods such as live baby brine shrimp, daphnia, or any other small, live food.

Breeding: Substrate spawner. Will breed in caves or on the sides of rocks or within caves. Offer juveniles live baby brine shrimp.

Name: *Lamprologus meleagris*
To 2¹/₂ inches (6 cm)

Distribution: Central Congo coastline over sandy areas in and near empty snail shells.

This **Lamprologus caudopunctatus** *from Kapampa, Congo, sports a yellow dorsal fin.*

Husbandry: Ideal Tanganyika cichlid to maintain in small aquariums of 10 gallons (38 L). Lay out several empty marine snail shells (provide one shell per fish) over a shallow layer of silica sand.

Diet: Microinvertebrates in the sand and zooplankton. Offer a variety of aquarium foods. Supplement the diet with live baby brine shrimp.

Breeding: Substrate-spawning shell dweller. Spawning occurs in female's shell. Male will defend the perimeter of the spawning site while the female guards the shell and babies. Offer juveniles live baby brine shrimp.

Name: *Lamprologus multifasciatus*
To 1¹/₂ inches (3.8 cm)

Distribution: Zambian coastline in sandy areas with empty snail shells from 35 to 80 feet (10.5–24 m) deep.

Husbandry: >5 gallons (19 L). Maintain over a shallow sandy bottom with one shell per individual. Can be kept with other peaceful Tanganyika cichlids.

Diet: Zooplankton. Offer a variety of aquarium foods. Supplement diet with live baby brine shrimp.

Breeding: Substrate spawner. Spawning will take place in female's shell and be guarded over by both parents. Male may spawn with several females within its territory. Offer juveniles live baby brine shrimp.

Lamprologus meleagris *is one of the more strikingly patterned shell-dwellers. Pictured is a male from the central Congo coastline.*

Lamprologus multifasciatus *is one of the smallest shell-dwellers from the lake.*

This Lamprologus ocellatus *male from Nkamba Bay, Zambia, is often referred to as the "Golden Ocellatus."*

Name: *Lamprologus ocellatus*
To 2 inches (5 cm)
    Distribution: Widespread in sandy areas with empty snail shells.
    Husbandry: Ideal cichlid for those with limited aquarium space. Can easily be maintained in aquariums as small as 10 gallons (38 L). One empty aquatic snail shell per individual should be provided along with a thin layer of silica sand.
    Diet: Sand-dwelling invertebrates and plankton. Offer a variety of aquarium foods. Supplement diet with aquatic brown worms.
    Breeding: Substrate spawner. Spawning takes place in female's shell. Male may spawn with more than a single female and provide protection at the perimeter of the territory. Offer juveniles live baby brine shrimp.

Name: *Lamprologus* sp. "Ornatipinnis Kigoma"
Males to 2³/₄ inches (6 cm), females to 1³/₄ inches (4.5 cm)
    Distribution: Northeast coastline at Kigoma. Inhabits shells over sandy plains
    Husbandry: >15 gallons (60 L). Maintain over fine sand, with one shell per individual. Maintain only to itself or with other peaceful species.
    Diet: Sand-dwelling invertebrates and zooplankton. Offer a variety of aquarium foods, sup-

plementing the diet with live and frozen brine shrimp and aquatic brown worms.
    Breeding: Substrate spawning shell-dweller. Will form a monogamous pair bond, and will chase away all other conspecifics. Spawns 10 to 15 eggs. Offer juveniles live baby brine shrimp.

Name: *Lamprologus similis*
To 1¹/₂ inches (3.8 cm)
    Distribution: Central coastline of the lake in Tanzania and Congo. Shell dwelling and rock dwelling over sandy/rocky areas from 35 to 100 feet (10.5–30 m) deep.
    Husbandry: >5 gallons (19 L). Maintain over a shallow sandy bottom with one shell per individual. Can be kept with other peaceful Tanganyika cichlids.

The undescribed Lamprologus sp. *"Ornatipinnis Kigoma" female is sitting guard near her nest.*

Lamprologus similis *is an ideal aquarium resident for small aquariums.*

Lamprologus speciosus *is a recently described shell-dweller confined to the central Congo coastline.*

Diet: Zooplankton. Offer a variety of aquarium foods. Supplement diet with live baby brine shrimp.

Breeding: Substrate spawner. Spawning will take place in female's shell and be guarded over by both parents. Male may spawn with several females within its territory. Offer juveniles live baby brine shrimp.

Name: *Lamprologus speciosus*
To 2½ inches (6 cm)
Distribution: Central Congo coastline over sandy areas in and near empty snail shells.

Husbandry: Ideal Tanganyikan cichlid to maintain in small aquariums of 10 gallons (38 L). Lay out several empty marine snail shells (provide one shell per fish) over a shallow layer of silica sand.

Diet: Microinvertebrates in the sand and zooplankton. Offer a variety of aquarium foods. Supplement the diet with live baby brine shrimp.

Breeding: Substrate-spawning shell dweller. Spawning occurs in female's shell. Male will defend the perimeter of the spawning site while the female guards the shell and babies. Offer juveniles live baby brine shrimp.

Name: *Lepidiolamprologus attenuatus*
To 6 inches (15 cm)
Distribution: Sandy/rocky areas to a depth of 100 feet (30 m).

Husbandry: >50 gallons (189 L). Several rocks should be provided to form caves and passageways. Only one male per aquarium is recommended—may not tolerate other males nearby. A skittish fish that needs a lot of hiding places.

Diet: Piscivore. Offer protein-rich foods such as fresh shrimp, feeder guppies, krill, and aquatic brown worms.

Lepidiolamprologus attenuatus *male from Cameron Bay, Zambia.*

This male **Lepidiolamprologus elongatus** *from Rutunga, Burundi, sports a darker brown body and fewer white spots than those variants from the southern part of the lake.*

This Zambian variant of L. elongatus *possesses a greater number of white spots on the body than the northern races.*

Breeding: Substrate spawner. Provide a cave for the female to lay its eggs in. May spawn so prolifically that the spawning pair may need to be separated. Offer juveniles live baby brine shrimp.

Name: *Lepidiolamprologus elongatus*
To 9 inches (23 cm)
Distribution: Widespread in rocky habitats.
Husbandry: >100 gallons (378.5 L). Husky, predatory cichlid best kept with other species with a similar disposition. Provide smooth stones piled up to form caves and passageways.

Diet: Piscivore. Offer a wide variety of high-quality aquarium foods. Supplement diet with high-protein foods.
Breeding: Substrate spawner. Will spawn on the side of a rock or in a cave. Clutch size averages 300 to 500 eggs. Both parents actively defend the spawning site against anything, including the hobbyist's hand! Offer juveniles live baby brine shrimp.

Name: *Lepidiolamprologus kendalli*
To 8 inches (20 cm)
Distribution: Southern area from Zambia to southern Tanzania. Inhabits rocky areas to a depth of 150 feet (45 m).
Husbandry: >75 gallons (283 L). Raise several juveniles in a community setup with similarly aggressive species. Provide extensive rock work, forming caves and passageways.
Diet: Piscivore. Offer a variety of meaty aquarium foods. Supplement diet with fresh-frozen or live shrimp and live feeder guppies.
Breeding: Substrate spawner. Pairs or trios may form with a single male servicing more than one female. Spawns in caves or other secluded structures. Offer juveniles live baby brine shrimp.

This **Lepidiolamprologus kendalli** *can be differentiated from* L. nkambae *by a scaled cheek, broader head, and a checkerboard color pattern.*

Name: *Lepidiolamprologus lemairii*
To 11 inches (28 cm)

Distribution: Widespread in all types of habitats from shallow water to a depth of 330 feet (99 m).

Husbandry: >75 gallons (283 L). Cryptic, ambushing piscivore; it will consume any fish small enough to fit into its mouth. Provide a shallow layer of silica sand and scattered rocks to serve as hiding places.

Diet: Piscivore. Offer meaty, high-protein foods such as fresh-frozen shrimp, earthworms, and live feeder guppies.

Breeding: Substrate spawner. Spawns in caves. Offer juveniles live baby brine shrimp.

Name: *Lepidiolamprologus meeli*
To 3 1/2 inches (9 cm)

Distribution: Southern half of the lake over shallow sandy area where empty snail shells are present.

Lepidiolamprologus meeli *male from Kalumbie, Congo.*

Lepidiolamprologus lemairii should not be maintained with any other species that will fit into its mouth.

Husbandry: >20 gallons (76 L). Provide one shell per individual over a sandy bottom.

Diet: Sand-dwelling invertebrates and zooplankton. Offer a variety of aquarium foods, supplementing the diet with live and frozen brine shrimp and aquatic brown worms.

Breeding: Substrate-spawning shell dweller. Dominant male may spawn with several females and may not tolerate any other male nearby. Offer juveniles live baby brine shrimp.

Name: *Lepidiolamprologus cf. meeli*
To 3 inches (7.6 cm)

Distribution: Central Congo coastline over shallow sandy area where empty snail shells are present.

Husbandry: >20 gallons (76 L). Provide one shell per individual over a sandy bottom.

Diet: Sand-dwelling invertebrates and zooplankton. Offer a variety of aquarium foods, supplementing the diet with live and frozen brine shrimp and aquatic brown worms.

Lepidiolamprologus cf. meeli *from the central Congo coastline.*

Breeding: Substrate-spawning shell dweller. Dominant male will spawn with several females and may not tolerate any other male nearby. Offer juveniles live baby brine shrimp.

Name: *Lepidiolamprologus nkambae*
To 8 inches (20 cm)

Lepidiolamprologus nkambae *from Nkamba Bay, Zambia, is one of the most striking Lamprologines.*

Distribution: Southern area from Zambia to southern Tanzania. Inhabits rocky areas to a depth of 150 feet (45 m).

Husbandry: >75 gallons (283 L). Raise several juveniles in a community setup with similarly aggressive species. Provide extensive rock work, forming caves and passageways.

Diet: Piscivore. Offer a variety of meaty aquarium foods. Supplement diet with fresh-frozen or live shrimp and live feeder guppies.

Breeding: Substrate spawner. Pairs or trios may form with a single male servicing more than one female. Spawns in caves or other secluded structures. Offer juveniles live baby brine shrimp.

Name: *Lepidiolamprologus pleuromaculatus*
To 5 inches (13 cm)

Distribution: Extreme northern end of the lake in Burundi and the northern Congo coastline, over sandy/rocky areas from 15 to 140 feet (4.5–42 m) deep.

Husbandry: >50 gallons (189 L). Provide several rocks piled up to form caves and passageways. Best maintained with other Lamprogolines in a community setup.

Diet: Fish and microinvertebrates. Offer high-protein aquarium foods such as live feeder guppies and fresh-frozen shrimp.

Breeding: Substrate spawner. Prefers to spawn in artificial caves. Spawn site guarded by both parents. Offer juveniles live baby brine shrimp.

Name: *Lepidiolamprologus profundicola*
To 18 inches (46 cm)

Distribution: Widespread over sandy/rocky areas from 15 to 330 feet (4.5–99 m) deep.

Husbandry: >150 gallons (568 L). Provide several rocks piled up to form caves and passageways. Best maintained with other Lamprogolines at least two-thirds their size.

Diet: Piscivore. Offer high-protein aquarium foods such as live feeder guppies and fresh-frozen shrimp.

Lepidiolamprologus pleuromaculatus *from Burundi has virtually vanished from the hobby.*

Lepidiolamprologus profundicola is the largest Lamprologine, reaching a length of nearly 18 inches (45 cm).

Breeding: Substrate spawner. Spawns in the open on a large rock. Spawn site guarded by both parents. No other fish should be present when spawning occurs, because they will be killed. Offer juveniles live baby brine shrimp.

Name: *Lepidiolamprologus* sp. "Profundicola Tanzania"
To 8 inches (20 cm)
Distribution: Tanzanian coastline from Kipili to Fulwe Rocks in rocky habitats.
Husbandry: >100 gallons (378.5 L). Predatory cichlid best kept with other species with a similar disposition. Provide smooth stones piled up to form caves and passageways.
Diet: Piscivore. Offer a wide variety of high-quality aquarium foods. Supplement diet with high-protein foods.
Breeding: Substrate spawner. Will spawn on the side of a rock or in a cave. Both parents actively defend the spawning site against all other fish. Offer juveniles live baby brine shrimp.

Name: *Lestradea perspicax*
To 5 inches (13 cm)
Distribution: Widespread in shallow sandy areas.

Subadults Lepidiolamprologus *sp.* "Profundicola Tanzania" *are known to school with and mimic* Cyprichromis *and* Paracyprichromis *species in order to prey upon them.*

Husbandry: >40 gallons (151 L). A peaceful species best maintained in groups of at least six. Maintain only with other peaceful Tanganyika cichlids.
Diet: Algae and diatoms. Offer a variety of commercially prepared aquarium foods. Small live or frozen foods should be regularly offered.

Lestradea perspicax *male from Rutunga, Burundi.*

Limnochromis auritus is an active digger that prefers sand in order to bring out its natural digging behavior.

Breeding: Maternal mouthbrooder. Should be the dominant species or only cichlid species in the aquarium if spawning is to occur. Eggs develop in 16 days. Offer juveniles live baby brine shrimp.

Name: *Limnochromis auritus*
To 8 inches (20 cm)
Distribution: Throughout the lake over muddy bottoms from 30 to 400 feet (9–120 m) deep.
Husbandry: >75 gallons (283 L). A peaceful species that digs a lot. Best maintained with other, less-aggressive Tanganyikan mouthbrooders.
Diet: Sand/mud-dwelling invertebrates and mollusks. Offer a variety of high-protein aquarium foods.
Breeding: Biparental mouthbrooder. Female begins brooding process for 8 to 11 days, then male finishes incubating period. Offer juveniles live baby brine shrimp.

Name: *Lobochilotes labiatus*
To 16 inches (40.6 cm)
Distribution: Throughout the lake in all kinds of habitats in shallow water.

Husbandry: Exceedingly aggressive species toward its own kind. Aquarium should be at least 250 gallons (946 L) if more than one is maintained together. Provide plenty of rocks piled up to form caves and passageways.
Diet: Mollusks and macroinvertebrates. Offer a wide variety of aquarium foods.
Breeding: Maternal mouthbrooder. Because of its aggressive tendencies towards its own kind, the divider method is recommended. Place a male on one side of the divider (firmly secured egg crate) and a female on other side. Spawning should take place between the vented divider. Offer juveniles live baby brine shrimp.

Name: *Microdontochromis tenuidentatus*
To 3¹/₂ inches (9 cm)
Distribution: Throughout the lake in all kinds of habitats in shallow water.
Husbandry: >30 gallons (113.5 L). A peaceful species best kept among themselves in groups of at least eight, over a sandy-bottomed aquarium with few smooth stones.
Diet: Zooplankton and phytoplankton. Offer a wide variety of aquarium foods. Supplement the diet with live baby brine shrimp and spirulina flake food.

Lobochilotes labiatus is an extremely aggressive species toward its own kind.

Microdontochromis tenuidentatus *is a great beginners' species to keep.*

Neolamprologus bifasciatus *produces small spawns every couple of weeks.*

Neolamprologus brichardi *is the most popular and recognizable cichlid from the lake. Pictured is a male from Burundi.*

Breeding: Maternal mouthbrooder. Spawning will take place when a male and female separate themselves from their school and spawn over the sand. Brooding female will rejoin school to incubate the eggs. Offer juveniles live baby brine shrimp.

Name: *Neolamprologus bifasciatus*
To 5 inches (13 cm).

Distribution: Widespread in rocky areas deeper than 120 feet (36 m).

Husbandry: >30 gallons (113.5 L). Established pairs may be kept in somewhat smaller aquariums. Provide plenty of rocks to form caves and passageways.

Diet: Microinvertebrates. Offer high-protein foods, whether dried or frozen. Supplement the diet with live aquatic brown worms and brine shrimp.

Breeding: Substrate spawner. A cave-spawning species that should be provided several caves. Spawns are small, and parents may spawn every two weeks. Offer juveniles live baby brine shrimp.

Name: *Neolamprologus brichardi*
To 4 inches (10 cm)

Distribution: Widespread in rocky areas down to 50 feet (15 m).

Husbandry: >15 gallons (57 L). Extensive colonies can be established in large aquariums >150 gallons (568 L) and larger with several pairs and schools of juveniles present.

Diet: Zooplanktivore. Offer a variety of aquarium foods. Supplemented diet with live baby brine shrimp and/or daphnia.

Breeding: A substrate spawner. Provide each spawning pair with a cave. Larger juveniles aid the parents in defending smaller juveniles. Offer juveniles live baby brine shrimp.

Neolamprologus buescheri from Cape Kachese, Zambia.

Neolamprologus cunningtoni darken considerably when in spawning mode.

Name: *Neolamprologus buescheri*
To 4 inches (10 cm)

Distribution: Southern coastline between Samazi, Tanzania, and Moba, Zaire. Inhabits rocky areas from 50 to 150 feet (15–45 m) deep.

Husbandry: >20 gallons (76 L), provided only one pair is present. Several individuals raised together will need an aquarium of at least 75 gallons (283 L). Provide ample hiding places and territories with several rocks piled up to form caves.

Diet: Microinvertebrates. Offer a variety of high-protein aquarium foods such as mysis shrimp and live aquatic brown worms.

Breeding: Substrate spawner. Provide caves and other secluded structures as spawning sites. Offer juveniles live baby brine shrimp.

Name: *Neolamprologus cunningtoni*
To 12 inches (30 cm)

Distribution: Widespread over sandy areas from 20 to 180 feet (6–55 m) deep.

Husbandry: >150 gallons (568 L). Provide plenty of sand and a few smooth stones evenly scattered. Will consume any other fish that can fit into its mouth.

Diet: Piscivore. Offer a variety of aquarium foods, including live aquatic brown worms, brine shrimp, and mysis shrimp.

Breeding: Substrate spawner. Best maintained as a single pair to itself in a large aquarium. Offer juveniles live baby brine shrimp.

Name: *Neolamprologus cylindricus*
To 5 inches (13 cm)

Distribution: Southern Tanzanian coastline down to Zambia at a depth of 20 to 80 feet (6–24 m).

Husbandry: >75 gallons (283 L). Provide plenty of rocks piled up to form passageways and caves. Do not maintain this species with the more delicate Tanganyika cichlids.

Neolamprologus cylindricus male from Malasa, Tanzania.

This gigantic 8-inch (20 cm) **Neolamprologus** *sp. "Eseki" from Burundi is easily told apart from species of the mondabu/modestus complex by its strongly lyrate tail.*

Diet: Microinvertebrates. Offer a variety of aquarium foods, including live aquatic brown worms, brine shrimp, and mysis shrimp.

Breeding: Substrate spawner. Provide caves or piles of rocks as a spawning site. May become overly aggressive toward other tankmates while protecting their young if aquarium is too small. Offer juveniles live baby brine shrimp.

Name: *Neolamprologus* sp. "Eseki"
To 8 inches (20 cm)
Distribution: From Rutunga, Burundi, to Mpimbwe, Tanzania, in shallow sandy/rocky areas less than 50 feet (15 m) deep.
Husbandry: >100 gallons (378.5 L). An aggressive species. Provide plenty of rocks piled up to form caves and passageways.
Diet: Microinvertebrates and small fish. Offer a variety of aquarium foods, including live aquatic brown worms, brine shrimp, and mysis shrimp.
Breeding: Substrate spawner. Provide caves or piles of rocks as a spawning site. May become

overly aggressive toward other tankmates while protecting their young if aquarium is too small. Offer juveniles live baby brine shrimp.

Name: *Neolamprologus falcicula*
To 3^1/$_2$ inches (9 cm)
Distribution: Central Tanzanian coastline from 15 to 100 feet (4.5–30 m) deep.
Husbandry: >50 gallons (189 L). Provide plenty of rocks piled up to form caves and passageways.
Diet: Microinvertebrates. Offer a variety of aquarium foods, including live aquatic brown worms, brine shrimp, and mysis shrimp.
Breeding: Substrate spawner. Provide caves or piles of rocks as a spawning site. May become overly aggressive toward other tankmates while protecting their young if aquarium is too small. Offer juveniles live baby brine shrimp.

Name: *Neolamprologus furcifer*
To 7 inches (18 cm)
Distribution: Widespread in shallow rocky areas, in and among large boulders.

Neolamprologus falcicula *from Nkondwe, Tanzania, was originally sold as* **Lamprologus** *sp. "Cygnus."*

Neolamprologus furcifer *male from Burundi.*

Husbandry: >100 gallons (378.5 L). Plenty of rocks should be piled up to form numerous caves and passageways. Highly aggressive species toward its own kind. Maintain with other aggressive Tanganyika cichlids.

Diet: Microinvertebrates and small fish. Offer high-protein foods such as fresh-frozen shrimp, live feeder guppies, and aquatic brown worms.

Breeding: Substrate spawner. Provide a cave with an entrance big enough for only the female to enter. If not enough shelter is provided, the male may kill the female. Offer juveniles live baby brine shrimp.

Name: *Neolamprologus gracilis*
To 3^1/2 inches (9 cm)

Distribution: Central Tanzanian coastline and at Kapampa, Congo, from 20 to 80 feet (6–24 m) deep.

Husbandry: >50 gallons (189 L). Provide plenty of rocks piled up to form caves and passageways. A peaceful species; maintain only with other mild mannered species.

Diet: Microinvertebrates. Offer a variety of aquarium foods, including live aquatic brown worms, brine shrimp, and mysis shrimp.

Breeding: Substrate spawner. Provide caves or piles of rocks as a spawning site. May become

somewhat aggressive toward other tankmates while protecting their young if aquarium is too small. Offer juveniles live baby brine shrimp.

Name: *Neolamprologus helianthus*
To 3^1/2 inches (8.5 cm)

Distribution: West coast near Kitumba, Congo over rocky areas in water from 30 to 80 feet (9 to 24 m) deep.

Husbandry: >40 gallons (151 L). Pairs may be managed in smaller aquariums. Provide plenty rocks to form caves and passageways.

Neolamprologus gracilis *male from Lyamembe, Tanzania.*

A male **Neolamprologus helianthus** *from Kijumba, Congo.*

Neolamprologus kungweensis is a very aggressive dwarf Lamprologine. Pictured is a female.

Diet: Microinvertebrates. Offer a variety of aquarium foods high in carotene to promote the yellow/orange highlights.

Breeding: Substrate spawner preferring caves. Spawns are usually small, and parents may spawn repeatedly every 15 days or so. Offer juveniles live baby brine shrimp.

Name: *Neolamprologus kungweensis*
To 2 inches (5 cm)
Distribution: Central eastern and western coastlines over shallow muddy areas, living in small holes dug into the substrate.

Husbandry: >50 gallons (76 L). Provide short pieces of PVC piping half buried in the sand per individual.

Diet: Sand-dwelling invertebrates and zooplankton. Offer a variety of aquarium foods, supplementing the diet with live and frozen brine shrimp and aquatic brown worms.

Breeding: Substrate-spawning mud burrower. Dominant male will spawn with several females and may not tolerate any other male nearby. Offer juveniles live baby brine shrimp.

Name: *Neolamprologus laparogramma*
To 2^1/2 inches (6 cm)
Distribution: Southern area around Isanga, Zambia, in sandy/muddy areas.

Husbandry: >10 gallons (37.8 L). Provide small caves, such as small pieces of PVC piping, along with a thin layer of silica sand.

Diet: Sand-dwelling invertebrates and plankton. Offer a variety of aquarium foods. Supplement diet with aquatic brown worms.

Breeding: Substrate spawner. In the wild, spawning takes place in female's tunnel. Male may spawn with more than a single female and provide protection at the perimeter of the territory. Offer juveniles live baby brine shrimp.

Name: *Neolamprologus leleupi*
To 4^1/2 inches (11 cm)
Distribution: Uvira, Congo, between the Malagarasi River and Bulu Point, Tanzania, and in

Neolamprologus laparogramma from Isanga, Zambia, is one of the newest dwarf lamprologines to be described.

It is difficult to find a more brilliantly colored cichlid from the lake than this **Neolamprologus leleupi** *from Karilani, Tanzania.*

southern Congo, between Cape Tembwe and Zongwe at a depth of 30 to 120 feet (9–36.5 m).

Husbandry: >75 gallons (283 L). Pairs may be managed in smaller aquariums. Provide plenty of rocks to form caves and passageways.

Diet: Microinvertebrates. Offer a variety of aquarium foods high in carotene to promote the yellow/orange coloration.

Breeding: Substrate spawner preferring caves. From day one, juveniles should be fed live baby brine shrimp exclusively and raised over a light substrate to assure correct color development.

Name: *Neolamprologus longicaudatus*
To 6 inches (15 cm)

Distribution: Ubwari Peninsula to the Kavalla Islands along the Congo shoreline from 35 to 80 feet (10.5–24 m) deep in rocky areas.

Husbandry: >100 gallons (378.5 L). Pile up plenty of rocks to form caves and passageways. Established pairs will not tolerate their own kind in the same aquarium unless maintained in a mixed community of large Lamprologines.

Diet: Microinvertebrates. Offer a variety of aquarium foods. Supplement diet with live adult brine shrimp, daphnia, and fresh-frozen shrimp.

Breeding: Substrate spawner. Prefers to spawn in caves. Offer juveniles live baby brine shrimp.

Name: *Neolamprologus marunguensis*
To 3½ inches (9 cm)

Distribution: Southern Congo coastline from Kapampa to Moliro at a depth of 20 to 80 feet (6–24 m).

Husbandry: >50 gallons (189 L). Provide plenty of rocks piled up to form passageways and caves.

Subadult **Neolamprologus longicaudatus** *from the Ubwari Peninsula, Congo.*

Neolamprologus marunguensis *from Kapampa, Congo, is one of the more peaceful species of the Brichardi complex.*

Neolamprologus mustax **male from Mpulungu, Zambia.**

Diet: Microinvertebrates. Offer a variety of aquarium foods, including live aquatic brown worms, brine shrimp, and mysis shrimp.

Breeding: Substrate spawner. Provide caves or piles of rocks as a spawning site. May become overly aggressive toward other tankmates while protecting their young if aquarium is too small. Offer juveniles live baby brine shrimp

Name: *Neolamprologus mustax*
To 3^1/$_2$ inches (9 cm)

Distribution: Zambian and southern Congo coastline in rocky areas from 15 to 80 feet (4.5–24 m) deep.

Husbandry: >40 gallons (151 L). Provide plenty of rocks piled up to form caves and passageways. Do not maintain with other aggressive Lamprologines.

Diet: Microinvertebrates. Offer a variety of aquarium foods, including carotene-rich foods to maintain the attractive yellow color.

Breeding: Substrate spawner. Prefers to spawn in seculed places such as caves. Offer juveniles live baby brine shrimp.

Name: *Neolamprologus* sp. "Mustax Moliro"
To 3^1/$_2$ inches (9 cm)

Distribution: Southern Congo/Zambian border, in rocky areas from 15 to 80 feet (4.5–24 m) deep

Husbandry: >40 gallons (151 L). Provide plenty of rocks piled up to form caves and passageways. Do not maintain with other aggressive Lamprologines.

Diet: Microinvertebrates. Offer a variety of aquarium foods.

Breeding: Substrate spawner. Prefers to spawn in secluded places such as caves. Offer juveniles live baby brine shrimp.

Name: *Neolamprologus niger*
To 3^1/$_2$ inches (9 cm)

Distribution: Northern Congo coastline and along the central Tanzanian coastline at Bulu Point. Inhabits rocky areas from 20 to 150 feet (6–45 m) deep.

Husbandry: >60 gallons (227 L), but established pairs can be maintained in >15 gallons

Neolamprologus **sp. *"Mustax Moliro"* differs from N. mustax *in that the eye and mouth are noticeably larger than in* N. mustax.**

Neolamprologus niger from Bulu, Tanzania. Subadult male.

(57 L). Provide plenty of rocks and artificial caves.

Diet: Microinvertebrates. Offer a variety of aquarium foods high in protein.

Breeding: Substrate spawner. Secretive cave spawner. Will produce small spawns every 10 to 15 days. Offer juveniles live baby brine shrimp.

Name: *Neolamprologus nigriventris*
To 4 1/2 inches (11 cm)

Distribution: West coast at Kiku, Congo (formerly Zaire). Inhabits rocky areas from 20 to 100 feet (6–30 m) deep.

Husbandry: Aggressive species that should be provided with a large aquarium of at least 75 gallons (283 L) and much rock work.

Neolamprologus nigriventris male from Kiku, Congo.

Diet: Microinvertebrates. Offer a variety of high-protein aquarium foods.

Breeding: Substrate spawner. Prefers to spawn in secretive places and should be provided with an artificial cave and/or rocks piled up to form caves and passageways. Offer juveniles live baby brine shrimp.

Name: *Neolamprologus obscurus*
To 4 inches (10 cm)

Distribution: Southern Congo, Zambian, and southern Tanzanian shoreline in rocky areas at depths of approximately 10 to 100 feet (3–30 m) deep.

Husbandry: >50 gallons (189 L). A mild-mannered species. Provide plenty of rocks arranged to form caves and passageways. Do not maintain with any fish small enough to fit into its mouth.

Diet: Microinvertebrates. Offer a variety of high-protein aquarium foods such as fresh shrimp and live aquatic brown worms.

Breeding: Substrate spawner. Prefers to spawn in secretive, secluded areas. Provide rocks and

Neolamprologus obscurus possesses a cryptic color pattern, commonly seen in small, shy rock-dwelling Lamprologines from the lake.

Neolamprologus prochilus *male from Mbete, Zambia. Note the unique, large, slinglike jaw.*

Husbandry: Gregarious. Can be kept in groups of eight in aquariums as small as 50 gallons (189 L), and pairs can be maintained in aquariums as small as 15 gallons (57 L). Rocks or artificial caves should be provided.

Diet: Zooplankton. Offer a variety of aquarium foods. Supplement diet with live baby brine shrimp.

Breeding: Substrate spawner. Will form spawning colonies if given the opportunity. Juveniles of various sizes are tolerated within the spawning site. Offer juveniles live baby brine shrimp.

Name: *Neolamprologus savoryi*
To 4 inches (10 cm)

Distribution: Widespread in rocky areas from 15 to 120 feet (4.5–36 m) deep.

Husbandry: >50 gallons (189 L). Provide plenty of rocks and some artificial caves.

artificial caves. Offer juveniles live baby brine shrimp.

Name: *Neolamprologus prochilus*
To 6 inches (15 cm)

Distribution: Zambian shoreline in rocky areas at depths of approximately 10 to 150 feet (3–45 m) deep.

Husbandry: >50 gallons (189 L). A mild-mannered species. Provide plenty of rocks arranged to form caves and passageways. Do not maintain with any fish small enough to fit into its mouth.

Diet: Fish and microinvertebrates. Offer a variety of high-protein aquarium foods such as live feeder guppies and live aquatic brown worms.

Breeding: Substrate spawner. Prefers to spawn in secretive, secluded areas. Provide rocks and artificial caves. Offer juveniles live baby brine shrimp.

Name: *Neolamprologus pulcher*
To 4 inches (10 cm)

Distribution: Southern part of the lake from western shoreline at Tembwe and Kalila on the eastern shoreline in Tanzania, southward into Zambia. Inhabits rocky areas from 15 to 50 feet (4.5–15 m) deep.

This color variant of **Neolamprologus pulcher** *hails from Kabwimba, Zambia, and is known in the hobby as the "Daffodil."*

Neolamprologus savoryi *male from Burundi.*

Neolamprologus sexfasciatus *from Kipili, Tanzania. Only the yellow variant of this species has so far reproduced in captivity.*

Somewhat scrappy; maintain only with other aggressive Lamprologines.

Diet: Microinvertebrates. Offer a variety of commercially prepared aquarium foods. Supplement the diet with live or frozen daphnia, brine shrimp, or mosquito larvae.

Breeding: Substrate spawner that prefers caves. Artificial caves and piled rocks are recommended. Offer juveniles live baby brine shrimp.

Name: *Neolamprologus sexfasciatus*
To 6 inches (15 cm)

Distribution: Southern half of the lake in sandy/rocky areas in water no deeper than 50 feet (15 m).

Husbandry: >100 gallons (378.5 L). Provide plenty of rocks piled up to form caves and passageways. Individual specimens can be maintained in a community setting with species of similar temperament.

Diet: Small fish and mollusks. Offer a variety of high-protein foods such as fresh-frozen shrimp, live feeder guppies, frozen clams, mussels, and ocean plankton.

Breeding: Substrate spawner. Only the yellow variant has been spawned in captivity. Provide several caves for the pair to choose from. Offer live baby brine shrimp to maintain the yellow coloration.

Name: *Neolamprologus signatus*
To 2½ inches (6 cm)

Distribution: Southwestern Zambian shoreline in sandy/muddy regions.

Husbandry: >10 gallons (37.8 L). Provide small caves, such as small pieces of PVC piping, along with a thin layer of silica sand.

Diet: Sand-dwelling invertebrates and plankton. Offer a variety of aquarium foods. Supplement diet with aquatic brown worms.

A male Neolamprologus signatus *from Tanzania.*

The yellow variant of **Neolamprologus tetracanthus** *from Kipili, Tanzania.*

Breeding: Substrate spawner. Spawning takes place in female's tunnel. Male may spawn with more than a single female and provide protection at the perimeter of the territory. Offer juveniles live baby brine shrimp.

Name: *Neolamprologus tetracanthus*
To 8 inches (20 cm)
Distribution: Widespread over shallow sandy/rocky areas.
Husbandry: >50 gallons (189 L). Provide an even array of rocks and sand to help demarcate territories. Can be maintained with other substrate-spawning Tanganyika cichlids of similar disposition.
Diet: Sand-dwelling invertebrates, small fishes, and mollusks. Offer a variety of high-protein aquarium foods, such as feeder guppies, fresh shrimp, and aquatic brown worms.
Breeding: Substrate spawner. Not fussy about spawning site. Provide rocks piled up to form caves and secluded areas. Both parents vigorously defend eggs, juveniles, and the spawning site against all intruders. Offer juveniles live baby brine shrimp.

Name: *Neolamprologus toae*
To 4 inches (10 cm)
Distribution: Northern half of the lake, except Burundi, over sandy/rocky areas from 15 to 50 feet (4.5–15 m) deep.
Husbandry: >50 gallons (189 L). A peaceful species. Provide plenty of shelter and open spaces. Cannot compete with the more aggressive Lamprologines.
Diet: Microinvertebrates. Offer a variety of aquarium foods. Supplement the diet with live or frozen daphnia, adult brine shrimp, and mosquito larvae.
Breeding: Substrate spawner. Pairs are quite tolerant of other fish near their spawning site. Artificial cave should be provided. Pair should be the dominant fish in the aquarium to trigger spawning. Offer juveniles live baby brine shrimp.

Name: *Neolamprologus tretocephalus*
To 6 inches (15 cm)
Distribution: Northern half of the lake in sandy/rocky areas from 15 to 50 feet (4.5–15 m) deep.
Husbandry: >100 gallons (378.5 L). Best maintained in a heavily rockscaped aquarium

Neolamprologus toae *from Toa, Congo.*

Neolamprologus tretocephalus *from Burundi.*

Neolamprologus *sp. "Ventralis Kasanga" male from Kasanga, Tanzania. This species differs from the* N. ventralis *by a deeper body and shorter ventral fins.*

with other Lamprologines of similar size and temperament.

Diet: Small fish and mollusks. Offer a variety of high-protein foods such as fresh-frozen shrimp, live feeder guppies, frozen clams, mussels, and ocean plankton.

Breeding: Substrate spawner. Provide a cave for spawning. Pair should be the only fish in the aquarium. All others will not be tolerated. Offer juveniles live baby brine shrimp.

Name: *Neolamprologus* sp. "Ventralis Kasanga"
To 3¹/₂ inches (9 cm)

Distribution: Zambian shoreline in sandy/rocky areas from 100 to 150 feet (30–45 m) deep.

Husbandry: >20 gallons (76 L). A placid species. Maintain a small group in a heavily rockscaped aquarium all to themselves.

Diet: Microinvertebrates. Offer a variety of high-protein foods such as live or frozen brine shrimp, mysis shrimp, bloodworms, and live aquatic brown worms.

Breeding: Substrate cave spawner. Provide a cave for spawning. Pair should be the only fish

in the aquarium. Will produce small spawns of approximately 30 eggs every two weeks. Offer juveniles live baby brine shrimp.

Name: *Neolamprologus* sp. "Walteri"
To 3¹/₂ inches (9 cm)

Distribution: Kigoma, Tanzania, from 15 to 100 feet (4.5–30 m) deep.

Husbandry: >50 gallons (189 L). Provide plenty of rocks piled up to form caves and passageways.

Neolamprologus *sp. "Walteri" from Kigoma differs from* N. falcicula *in having a deeper body, larger scales, and unique fin patterning.*

Ophthalmotilapia boops *male from Kipili, Tanzania.*

Diet: Microinvertebrates. Offer a variety of aquarium foods, including live aquatic brown worms, brine shrimp, and mysis shrimp.

Breeding: Substrate spawner. Provide caves or piles of rocks as a spawning site. May become overly aggressive toward other tankmates while protecting their young if aquarium is too small. Offer juveniles live baby brine shrimp.

Name: *Ophthalmotilapia boops*
To 6 inches (15 cm)

Distribution: Eastern shoreline in Tanzania, from Msalaba to Hinde B in sandy/rocky areas from near the surface to 25 feet (1–7 m) deep.

Husbandry: >75 gallons (283 L). Maintain one male per several females. Provide a few smooth stones and a shallow layer of silica sand.

Diet: Zooplankton and phytoplankton. Offer commercially prepared aquarium foods. Supplement the diet with spirulina-based foods.

Breeding: Maternal mouthbrooder. Dominant male will construct a sand nest as a spawning site. Brooding female(s) should be isolated from the overly aggressive male. Eggs develop in 21 days. Offer juveniles live baby brine shrimp.

Name: *Ophthalmotilapia nasuta*
To 8 inches (20 cm)

Distribution: Widespread wherever rocky areas are present, to a depth of 50 feet (15 m).

Husbandry: >100 gallons (378.5 L). Maintain one male per several females. Provide a few smooth stones and a shallow layer of silica sand.

Diet: Zooplankton and phytoplankton. Offer commercially prepared aquarium foods. Supplement the diet with spirulina-based foods.

Breeding: Maternal mouthbrooder. Dominant male will construct a sand nest as a spawning site. Brooding female(s) should be isolated from the overly aggressive male. Eggs develop in 21 days. Offer juveniles live baby brine shrimp.

Name: *Ophthalmotilapia ventralis*
To 6 inches (15 cm)

Distribution: Widespread, except in the northen part of the lake in Burundi and Congo north of the Ubwari Peninsula wherever rocky areas are present, from the surface to a depth of 50 feet (1 to 15 m).

Male **Ophthalmotilapia nasuta** *from Musoka, Congo.*

Ophthalmotilapia ventralis *male from Cape Chaitika, Zambia.*

Male **Paracyprichromis brieni** *from Kitumba, Congo.*

Husbandry: >75 gallons (283 L). Maintain one male per several females. Provide a few smooth stones and a shallow layer of silica sand.

Diet: Zooplankton and phytoplankton. Offer commercially prepared aquarium foods. Supplement the diet with spirulina-based foods.

Breeding: Maternal mouthbrooder. Dominant male will construct a sand nest as a spawning site. Brooding female(s) should be isolated from the overly aggressive male. Eggs develop in 21 days. Offer juveniles live baby brine shrimp.

Name: *Paracyprichromis brieni*
To 4 inches (10 cm)

Distribution: Widespread in open water near large boulders from 35 to 80 feet (10–24 m) deep.

Husbandry: >50 gallons (189 L). Maintain at least eight together in a tall aquarium with plenty of open space. Angle large pieces of slate upward to give the dominant males cavelike territories.

Diet: Zooplankton. Will eat most prepared aquarium foods small enough to fit into its mouth. Include live baby brine shrimp.

Breeding: Maternal mouthbrooder. Dominant male will stake out a territory in midwater and

proceed to coax any nearby female to spawn. Brooding females hold for approximately 21 days. Offer juveniles live baby brine shrimp.

Name: *Paracyprichromis nigripinnis*
To 4 inches (10 cm)

Distribution: Widespread at depths of 35 to 140 feet (10.5–42 m). Males are usually found upside down in caves. Females are found in large schools nearby.

Husbandry: Minimum 75 gallons (283 L). Maintain at least eight together in a tall aquarium with plenty of open space. Angle large pieces of slate upward to give the dominant males cavelike territories.

Paracyprichromis nigripinnis *male from Chituta Bay, Zambia.*

Diet: Zooplankton. Will eat most prepared aquarium foods small enough to fit into its mouth. Include live baby brine shrimp.

Breeding: Maternal mouthbrooder. Dominant male will stake out a territory in midwater and proceed to coax any nearby female to spawn. Brooding females hold for approximately 21 days. Offer juveniles live baby brine shrimp.

Name: *Perissodus microlepis*
To 5¹/₂ inches (13 cm)

Distribution: Throughout the lake over sandy/rocky areas from the surface to 50 feet (1–15 m) deep.

Husbandry: >100 gallons (378.5 L). Wild imports should be kept in isolation until they can be weaned onto commercially prepared aquarium foods. Once acclimated, rather peaceful and best maintained with other cichlids more aggressive than itself.

Diet: The scales of other cichlids. The few captive specimens imported were eventually weaned onto prepared aquarium foods.

Breeding: Biparental mouthbrooder. Female incubates eggs for first seven to ten days; then the male completes the incubative process. Offer juveniles live baby brine shrimp.

Petrochromis trewavasae *is one of the less aggressive* **Petrochromis** *species.*

Name: *Petrochromis trewavasae*
To 8 inches (20 cm)

Distribution: Throughout southwest coastline between Kapampa, Congo, and Katete, Zambia, in shallow, rocky areas.

Husbandry: >150 gallons (568 L). Provide plenty of rocks piled up to form caves and passageways. Best maintained in a community setup with species of a similar temperament.

Diet: Algae. Offer only dried or frozen foods specially designed for herbivores. Be careful not to overfeed.

Breeding: Maternal mouthbrooder. Male will court any responsive female. Eggs are large and take about 28 to 32 days to develop into free-swimming juveniles. If brooding female is overly harassed by male, remove male for duration of brooding period. Offer juveniles live baby brine shrimp and finely crushed spirulina flakes.

Perrisodus microlepis *is the most commonly encountered scale eater in the lake.*

Petrochromis sp. "Texas Tembwe" male from Tembwe, Congo.

Name: *Petrochromis* sp. " Texas Tembwe"
To 7 inches (18 cm)

Distribution: Southwest coastline at Tembwe, Congo, over rocky areas in shallow water.

Husbandry : >250 gallons (946 L). Very aggressive species toward its own kind. Male may be relentless in its pursuit of females in same aquarium. Best maintained in a community setup with no decorations or rocks, and with other aggressive mouthbrooding or substrate-spawning species.

Diet: Algae. Offer only dried or frozen foods specially designed for herbivores. Be careful not to overfeed.

Breeding: Because of its aggressive tendencies toward its own kind, the divider method is recommended. Place a male on one side of the divider (firmly secured egg crate), and a female on the other side. Spawning should take place between the vented divider. Offer juveniles live baby brine shrimp and finely crushed spirulina flakes.

Name: *Plecodus multidentatus*
To 8 inches (20 cm)

Distribution: Throughout the lake over sandy/rocky areas from 100 to 350 feet (30–105 m) deep.

Husbandry: >100 gallons (378.5 L). Wild imports should be kept in isolation until they can be weaned onto commercially prepared aquarium foods. Once acclimated, rather peaceful and best maintained with other cichlids more aggressive than itself.

Diet: The scales of other cichlids. The few captive specimens imported were easily weaned on to prepared aquarium food.

Breeding: Mouthbrooder. Has not yet reproduced in captivity.

Name: *Plecodus paradoxus*
To 12 inches (30 cm)

Distribution: Throughout the lake over sandy/rocky areas from 35 to 350 feet (10.5–105 m) deep.

Husbandry: >100 gallons (378.5 L). Wild imports should be kept in isolation until they can be weaned onto commercially prepared

Plecodus multidentatus may be a mimic of Benthochromis tricoti in the wild.

The scale eating **Plecodus paraxodus** *has been successfully weaned onto prepared aquarium foods in captivity.*

Plecodus straelini *is a* Cyphotilapia frontosa *and* C. gibberosa *mimic, enabling it to approach close enough undetected in order to eat their scales.*

aquarium foods. Once acclimated, rather peaceful and best maintained with other cichlids more aggressive than itself.

Diet: The scales of other cichlids. The few captive specimens imported were eventually weaned onto prepared aquarium foods.

Breeding: Biparental mouthbrooder. Female incubates eggs for first seven to ten days; then the male completes the incubative process. Offer juveniles live baby brine shrimp.

Name: *Plecodus straelini*
To 6 inches (15 cm)

Distribution: Throughout the lake over rocky areas from 10 to 70 feet (3–21 m) deep.

Husbandry: >100 gallons (378.5 L). Should be maintained by themselves until they can be weaned onto aquarium foods. Afterward rather peaceful and best maintained with other cichlids more aggressive than it is. Do not maintain with any species with a similar color pattern.

Diet: The scales of other cichlids that look similar to itself. The few captive specimens imported were eventually weaned onto prepared aquarium foods.

Breeding: Biparental mouthbrooder. Female incubates eggs for first seven to ten days; then the male completes the incubative process. Offer juveniles live baby brine shrimp.

Name: *Reganochromis calliurus*
To 6 inches (15 cm)

Distribution: Throughout the lake over muddy areas between 50 and 350 feet (15–105 m) deep.

Reganochromis calliurus *shows some subtle regional color variation, like this specimen from southern Congo, with a yellow marginal band on the dorsal fin.*

Husbandry: >50 gallons (189 L). A peaceful species, best kept over a layer of silica sand with a few smooth stones piled up to form caves. Do not maintain with aggressive Tanganyika cichlids

Diet: Sand-dwelling invertebrates. Offer a variety of aquarium foods such as live brine shrimp, daphnia, mosquito larvae, and live aquatic brown worms.

Breeding: Biparental mouthbrooder. Both parents will incubate the clutch of eggs at the same time. Offer juveniles live baby brine shrimp.

Name: *Simochromis pleurospilus*
To 4 inches (10 cm)

Distribution: Zambian and Congo coastline up to Kaleme, in shallow sandy/rocky areas with aquatic vegetation.

Husbandry: >75 gallons (283 L). Provide plenty of rocks in the form of caves and passageways. Can be kept in a community setup so long as the other aquarium inhabitants are not overly aggressive.

Diet: Algae. Offer frozen and dried foods specially designed for herbivores. Be careful not to overfeed.

Breeding: Maternal mouthbrooder. Male will court female within its territory. Males will spawn with multiple females if given the opportunity. Eggs and clutch size are usually small, and free-swimming juveniles should be offered live baby brine shrimp and finely crushed spirulina flakes.

Name: *Spathodus erythrodon*
To 3¹/₂ inches (9 cm)

Distribution: Throughout the northern half of the lake in the upper 10 feet (3 m) of the surf zone over small stones.

Husbandry: >40 gallons (151 L), heavily strewn with smooth rocks. Maintain in groups of at

This attractive color variant of **Simochromis pleurospilus** *hails from Zambian waters.*

least six. Provide moderate current with highly oxygenated water.

Diet: Algae. Offer foods high in spirulina and algae.

Breeding: Biparental mouthbrooder. Female incubates the eggs for approximately 11 days at first; then the embryos are transferred to the male, who incubates them for an additional 11 days. Offer juveniles live baby brine shrimp and finely crushed spirulina flakes.

Spathodus erythrodon *is the more attractive of the two species of "goby cichlids" found in the northern half of the lake.*

Telmatochromis brichardi *is often incorrectly referred to in the hobby as* T. bifrenatus.

Telmatochromis dhonti *from Kavalla, Congo.*

Telmatochromis sp. *"Temporalis Shell" from Sumbu, Zambia.*

Name: *Telmatochromis brichardi*
To 3 inches (7.6 cm)

Distribution: Southern half of the lake, as well as Burundi. Inhabits rocky areas in shallow water.

Husbandry: Peaceful species that can be maintained in aquariums no smaller than 10 gallons (38 L). Provide many rocks and small artificial caves.

Diet: Small aquatic invertebrates and the eggs of larger substrate-spawning cichlids. Offer a variety of aquarium foods.

Breeding: Substrate spawner. Will spawn in any secluded object offered. An ideal beginner's cichlid to maintain and spawn. Offer juveniles live baby brine shrimp.

Name: *Telmatochromis dhonti*
To 4 inches (10 cm)

Distribution: Widespread. Inhabits rocky areas in shallow water.

Husbandry: A moderately aggressive species that can be maintained in aquariums no smaller than 40 gallons (151 L). Provide many rocks and small, artificial caves.

Diet: Small aquatic invertebrates. Offer a variety of high-protein aquarium foods such as frozen brine shrimp, mysis shrimp, bloodworms, and live aquatic brown worms.

Breeding: Substrate spawner. Will spawn in any secluded object offered. Offer juveniles live baby brine shrimp.

Name: *Telmatochromis sp. "Temporalis Shell"*
To 2¹/₂ inches (6 cm)

Distribution: Southern half of the lake in empty snail shells over sandy areas from 25 to 80 feet (7.6–24 m) deep.

Husbandry: >20 gallons (76 L). One shell per individual is recommended. Maintain as a pair or in a mixed community setup with open-water-dwelling Tanganyika cichlids.

Diet: Sand-dwelling microinvertebrates and zooplankton. Offer a variety of aquarium foods. Supplement the diet with live baby brine shrimp.

Breeding: Substrate spawner. Spawning takes place within female's shell. Eggs and juveniles are protected by both parents. Offer juveniles live baby brine shrimp.

Name: *Telmatochromis vittatus*
To 4 inches (10 cm)

Distribution: Southern half of the lake. Inhabits rocky areas in shallow water.

Husbandry: Peaceful species that can be maintained in aquariums no smaller than 15 gallons (57 L). Provide many rocks and small artificial caves.

Diet: Small aquatic invertebrates and the eggs of larger substrate-spawning cichlids. Offer a variety of aquarium foods.

Breeding: Substrate spawner. Will spawn in any secluded object offered. An ideal beginner's cichlid to maintain and breed. Offer juveniles live baby brine shrimp.

Name: *Trematocara nigrifrons*
To 4¹/₂ inches (11 cm)

Distribution: Throughout the lake in open water near shore, from the surface at night to 500 feet (150 m) in the day.

Husbandry: >50 gallons (189 L). Delicate; should be kept to itself in groups of at least eight. Provide a layer of silica sand and one

Trematocara nigrifrons males develop a black throat when sexually aroused, and are smaller than females. Pictured is a male from Zambia.

Telmatochromis vittatus is a great beginners' cichlid because it is small and peaceful.

or two large, smooth stones. Lighting should be minimal.

Diet: Zooplankton, and opportunistic piscivore. Offer live baby and adult brine shrimp, mosquito larvae, daphnia, and live aquatic brown worms.

Breeding: Maternal mouthbrooder. Male may spawn with several females on the same day in its sand nest. Females will brood their eggs for 16 days. Offer juveniles live baby brine shrimp.

Name: *Trematocara stigmaticum*
To 3¹/₂ inches (9 cm)

Distribution: Throughout the lake in open water near shore, from the surface at night, to 500 feet (150 m) deep in the day.

Trematocara stigmaticum *male from Zambia.*

Trematocara marginatum *male from Zambia.*

Husbandry: >50 gallons (189 L). Delicate; should be kept to itself in groups of at least eight. Provide a layer of silica sand and one or two large smooth stones. Lighting should be minimal.

Diet: Zooplankton. Offer live baby and adult brine shrimp, mosquito larvae, daphnia, bloodworms, and live aquatic brown worms.

Breeding: Maternal mouthbrooder. Male may spawn with several females on the same day in its sand nest. Females will brood their eggs for 16 days. Offer juveniles live baby brine shrimp.

Name: *Trematocara marginatum*
To 4 inches (10 cm)

Distribution: Throughout the lake in open water near shore, from the surface at night, to 500 feet (150 m) deep in the day.

Husbandry: >50 gallons (189 L). Delicate; should be kept to itself in groups of at least eight. Provide a layer of silica sand and one or two large smooth stones. Lighting should be minimal.

Diet: Zooplankton. Offer live baby and adult brine shrimp, mosquito larvae, daphnia, bloodworms, and live aquatic brown worms.

Breeding: Maternal mouthbrooder. Male may spawn with several females on the same day in its sand nest. Females will brood their eggs for 16 days. Offer juveniles live baby brine shrimp.

Name: *Triglachromis otostigma*
To 5 inches (12.5 cm)

Distribution: Throughout the lake over muddy areas from 35 to 170 feet (10.5–51 m) deep.

Husbandry: >50 gallons (189 L). Provide PVC piping with one end buried in silica sand as a cave for dwelling and hiding.

Triglachromis otostigma *male from Burundi.*

Diet: Consumes diatoms found in the mud. Offer a variety of aquarium foods. Supplement diet with live baby brine shrimp.

Breeding: Biparental mouthbrooder. In the wild, a pair digs a tunnel in the muddy bottom and spawns in it. PVC tubing with silica sand piled over it will help digging activity and stimulate spawning.

Name: *Tropheus* sp. "Black"
To 5¹/₂ inches (14 cm)

Distribution: Throughout the northern half of the lake over shallow rocky areas.

Husbandry: >100 gallons (378.5 L). Advisable to maintain this species in groups of at least 15. Provide plenty of rocks piled up to form caves and passageways. Gravel or sand is not recommended. Large, regular water changes are a must for this species' long-term health.

Diet: Algae. Offer frozen and dried foods specially designed for herbivores. Be careful not to overfeed.

Breeding: Maternal mouthbrooder. Spawning will usually take place randomly in the aquarium, and the brooding female will rejoin the group after spawning has taken place. The incubation period lasts about 30 days, although the female may hold well beyond that time. Offer juveniles live baby brine shrimp and finely crushed spirulina flakes.

Name: *Tropheus brichardi*
To 5¹/₂ inches (14 cm)

Distribution: Central shoreline on both east and west coasts of the lake over shallow rocky areas.

Husbandry: >100 gallons (378.5 L). Advisable to maintain this species in groups of at least 15. Provide plenty of rocks piled up to form caves

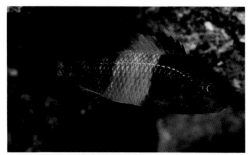

Tropheus sp. "Black" occurs in the northern half of the lake and comes in a vast array of geographical color variants. Pictured is a variant from Pemba, Congo.

This variant of Tropheus sp. "Black" hails from Kiriza, Congo.

Tropheus brichardi, such as this variant from Katonga, Tanzania, is more aggressive in captivity than other Tropheus species.

Juvenile Tropheus duboisi *display an attractive juvenile color pattern.*

and passageways. Gravel or sand is not recommended. Large, regular water changes are a
must for this species' long-term health.

Diet: Algae. Offer frozen and dried foods
specially designed for herbivores. Be careful not
to overfeed.

Breeding: Maternal mouthbrooder. Spawning
will usually take place randomly in the aquarium, and the brooding female will rejoin the
group after spawning has taken place. The
incubation period lasts for about 30 days,

although the female may hold well beyond
that time. Offer juveniles live baby brine shrimp
and finely crushed spirulina flakes.

Name: *Tropheus duboisi*
To 5 inches (13 cm).

Distribution: Northern portion of the lake at
various isolated locales in rocky areas from 15 to
50 feet (4.5–15 m) deep.

Husbandry: >50 gallons (189 L). Provide
plenty of rocks piled up to create caves and
passageways. A relatively peaceful *Tropheus*
species that is best maintained in groups of at
least ten.

Diet: Algae. Offer frozen and dried foods
specially designed for herbivores. Be careful not
to overfeed.

Breeding: Maternal mouthbrooder.
Spawning will take place in a secluded
area, and brooding female may rejoin
the group after spawning. Incubation
period lasts about 30 days, although
the female may hold well beyond that
time. Offer juveniles live baby brine
shrimp and finely crushed spirulina
flakes.

Name: *Tropheus* sp. "Ikola"
To 5$^{1}/_{2}$ inches (14 cm)

Distribution: Ikola, Tanzania, over
shallow rocky areas.

Husbandry: >100 gallons (378.5 L).
Advisable to maintain this species in

Adult T. duboisi *from Maswa, Tanzania.*

Tropheus *sp. "Ikola" male from Ikola, Tanzania.*

Tropheus moorii Murago, *from the Congo side of the lake.*

This unusual mutation of T. moorii *is from Kalambo, near the Tanzanian and Zambian borders.*

This variant of T. moorii *hails from Mpulungu, Zambia.*

groups of at least 15. Provide plenty of rocks piled up to form caves and passageways. Gravel or sand is not recommended. Large, regular water changes are a must for this species' long-term health.

Diet: Algae. Offer frozen and dried foods specially designed for herbivores. Be careful not to overfeed.

Breeding: Maternal mouthbrooder. Spawning will usually take place randomly in the aquarium, and the brooding female will rejoin the group after spawning has taken place. The incubation period lasts about 30 days, although the female may hold well beyond that time. Offer juveniles live baby brine shrimp and finely crushed spirulina flakes.

Name: *Tropheus moorii*
To 5¹/₂ inches (14 cm)

Distribution: Throughout the southern half of the lake over shallow rocky areas.

Husbandry: >100 gallons (378.5 L). Advisable to maintain this species in groups of at least 15. Provide plenty of rocks piled up to form caves and passageways. Gravel or sand is not recom-

Tropheus polli from Bulu Point, Tanzania. This is one of the more peaceful Tropheus species.

mended. Large, regular water changes are a must for this species' long-term health.

Diet: Algae. Offer frozen and dried foods specially designed for herbivores. Be careful not to overfeed.

Breeding: Maternal mouthbrooder. Spawning will usually take place randomly in the aquarium, and the brooding female will rejoin the group after spawning has taken place. The incubation period lasts for about 30 days, although the female may hold well beyond that time. Offer juveniles live baby brine shrimp and finely crushed spirulina flakes.

Name: *Tropheus polli*
To 5 1/2 inches (14 cm)

Distribution: On the east coast from Bulu Point to Sibwesa, in rocky areas from 20 to 60 feet (6–18 m) deep.

Husbandry: >50 gallons (189 L). Provide plenty of rocks piled up to create caves and passageways. A relatively peaceful *Tropheus* species that is best maintained in groups of at

least ten. In males, the tail becomes increasingly lyrate with age.

Diet: Algae. Offer frozen and dried foods specially designed for herbivores. Be careful not to overfeed.

Breeding: Maternal mouthbrooder. Spawning will usually take place randomly in the aquarium, and the brooding female will rejoin the group after spawning has taken place. The incubation period lasts about 30 days, although the female may hold well beyond that time. Offer juveniles live baby brine shrimp and finely crushed spirulina flakes.

Name: *Tylochromis polylepis*
To 14 inches (36 cm)

Distribution: Widespread in shallow water in sandy and muddy areas near river mouths.

Husbandry: >250 gallons (946 L) will be needed if more than one specimen is to be

Tylochromis polylepis is a consummate jumper, so take extra care to keep a tight lid on your aquarium.

housed together. If maintained singly with other species of Tanganyika cichlids, can be quite peaceful. Make sure lid of aquarium is secure, as this species is adept at jumping from the water.

Diet: Omnivorous. Offer a wide variety of aquarium foods, whether live or commercially prepared.

Breeding: Because of its aggressive tendencies toward its own kind, the divider method is recommended. Place a single male on one side of the divider (firmly secured egg crate) and a single female on the other side. Spawning should take place between vented divider; then brooding female can incubate her brood unmolested. Offer juveniles live baby brine shrimp.

Name: *Variabilichromis moorii*
To 5 inches (13 cm)

Distribution: Found throughout the northern half of the lake in shallow sandy/rocky areas.

Husbandry: >50 gallons (189 L). Provide plenty of rocks piled up to form caves and passageways. A slow-growing species, patience is required in raising it to maturity.

Diet: Zooplankton, phytoplankton, and sand-dwelling invertebrates. This species has a very long intestine (twice the length of the body), indicating a diet higher in vegetable matter than any other Lamprologine. Spirulina-based foods should supplement the diet.

Breeding: Substrate spawner. Prefers to spawn in caves. Juveniles may show a beautiful pastel yellow body. Offer juveniles live baby brine shrimp.

Variabilichromis moorii *male from Cameron Bay, Zambia.*

Name: *Xenotilapia flavipinnis*
To 4 inches (10 cm)

Distribution: Widspread in shallow sandy areas.

Husbandry: >40 gallons (151 L). Maintain in groups of at least eight. A mild-mannered species, not to be maintained with aggressive rock-dwelling substrate-spawners.

Diet: Sand-dwelling invertebrates. Offer a variety of aquarium foods. Supplement with live aquatic brown worms.

Breeding: Biparental mouthbrooder. A pair will separate from the group and spawn. The female

Xenotilapia flavipinnis *male from Katili, Tanzania.*

Xenotilapia sp. "Fluorescent Green" appears to be confined to Zambian waters.

initially broods the eggs for approximately ten days; then the larvae are transferred to the male, who will incubates them for five to six more days. Offer juveniles live baby brine shrimp.

Name: *Xenotilapia* sp. "Fluorescent Green"
To 4 inches (10 cm)
Distribution: Zambian shoreline in deep sandy areas from 80 to 150 feet (24 to 45 m) deep.
Husbandry: >50 gallons (189 L). Maintain in groups of at least eight. A mild-mannered species, not to be maintained with aggressive rock-dwelling substrate spawners.

Diet: Sand-dwelling invertebrates. Offer a variety of aquarium foods. Supplement the diet with live or frozen brine shrimp, live aquatic brown worms, and daphnia.
Breeding: Biparental mouthbrooder. The male will spawn with as many receptive females as possible within a nest constructed of five small heaps of sand in a circle. Eggs develop in 21 days. Offer juveniles live baby brine shrimp.

Name: *Xenotilapia nigrolabiata*
To 5 inches (13 cm)
Distribution: Chituta Bay, Zambia, in muddy/sandy areas from 150 to 200 feet (45–60 m) deep.
Husbandry: >50 gallons (189 L). Maintain in groups of at least eight over a shallow, sandy bottom without any rocks. Best to maintain with its own kind, as it is a very peaceful species.
Diet: Sand-dwelling invertebrates. Offer a variety of aquarium foods. Supplement the diet with live or frozen brine shrimp, live aquatic brown worms, and daphnia.
Breeding: Maternal mouthbrooder. Eggs develop in 18 days. Offer juveniles live baby brine shrimp.

Xenotilapia nigrolabiata aka "Red Princess" is the newest and most exciting Xenotilapia species to have been exported. Pictured is an adult male from Chituta Bay, Zambia.

Xenotilapia ochrogenys yawning male from Burundi.

Name: *Xenotilapia ochrogenys*
To 5 inches (13 cm)

Distribution: Widespread in shallow sandy areas.

Husbandry: >50 gallons (189 L). Maintain in groups of at least eight. A mild-mannered species, not to be maintained with aggressive rock-dwelling substrate spawners.

Diet: Sand-dwelling invertebrates. Offer a variety of aquarium foods. Supplement the diet with live or frozen brine shrimp, live aquatic brown worms, and daphnia.

Breeding: A lek-spawning maternal mouthbrooder. The male will spawn with as many receptive females as possible within a nest constructed of five small heaps of sand in a circle. Eggs develop in 21 days. Offer juveniles live baby brine shrimp.

Name: *Xenotilapia ornatipinnis*
To 5 inches (13 cm)

Distribution: Northern half of the lake in sandy areas from 35 to 200 feet (10.5–60 m) deep.

Husbandry: >50 gallons (189 L). Maintain in groups of at least eight over a shallow, sandy bottom without any rocks.

Diet: Sand-dwelling invertebrates. Offer a variety of aquarium foods. Supplement the diet with live or frozen brine shrimp, live aquatic brown worms, and daphnia.

Breeding: Maternal to biparental mouthbrooder. The transfer of embryos from a breeding male to a nonbreeding male has been observed. Eggs develop in 21 days. Offer juveniles live baby brine shrimp.

Name: *Xenotilapia* sp. "Papilio Sunflower"
To 4 inches (10 cm)

Distribution: Southern Tanzanian coastline to Chituta Bay, Zambia in sandy areas from 10 to 150 feet (3–45 m) deep.

Husbandry: >50 gallons (189 L). Maintain in groups of at least eight over a shallow, sandy bottom without any rocks. Best maintained among its own kind.

Diet: Sand-dwelling invertebrates. Offer a variety of aquarium foods. Supplement the diet with live or frozen brine shrimp, live aquatic brown worms, and daphnia.

Xenotilapia ornatipinnis is one of the more attractive deep water species made available to the hobby.

Xenotilapia sp. "Papilio Sunflower" male from Kalambo, near the Tanzanian and Zambian borders.

Breeding: Biparental mouthbrooder. Eggs develop in 21 days. Offer juveniles live baby brine shrimp.

Name: *Xenotilapia singularis*
To 5 inches (13 cm)
Distribution: Zambian coastline in shallow sandy areas.
Husbandry: >50 gallons (189 L). Maintain in groups of at least eight. A mild-mannered

species, not to be maintained with aggressive rock-dwelling substrate spawners.
Diet: Sand-dwelling invertebrates. Offer a variety of aquarium foods. Supplement the diet with live or frozen brine shrimp, live aquatic brown worms, and daphnia.
Breeding: A lek-spawning maternal mouthbrooder. The male will spawn with as many receptive females as possible within a nest constructed of five small heaps of sand in a circle. Eggs develop in 21 days. Offer juveniles live baby brine shrimp.

Name: *Xenotilapia spilopterus*
To 5 inches (13 cm)
Distribution: Southern half of the lake in sandy/rocky areas from 20 to 60 feet (6–18 m) deep.
Husbandry: >50 gallons (189 L). Maintain in groups of at least eight over a shallow, sandy bottom without any rocks.

Xenotilapia singularis, formerly known as "Ndole Bay Ochrogenys," is confined to Zambian waters.

Xenotilapia spilopterus occurs in a multitude of color variants throughout the lake. Pictured is a male from Kipili, Tanzania.

This X. spilopterus *hails from Ndole Bay, Zambia.*

Diet: Sand-dwelling invertebrates. Offer a variety of aquarium foods. Supplement the diet with live or frozen brine shrimp, live aquatic brown worms, and daphnia.

Breeding: Biparental mouthbrooder. Eggs develop in 16 days. Offer juveniles live baby brine shrimp.

New Genus? Species unknown
To 6 inches (15 cm)
Distribution: Chituta Bay over muddy bottom areas from 150 feet (45 m) deep.

Husbandry: >100 gallons (378.5 L). Maintain in groups of at least eight over a shallow, sandy bottom without any rocks, similar to Cyathopharynx/Cunningtonia species.

Diet: Sand-dwelling invertebrates. Offer a variety of aquarium foods. Supplement the diet with live or frozen brine shrimp, live aquatic brown worms, and daphnia.

Breeding: Maternal(?) mouthbrooder. Has yet to spawn in captivity.

I trust that this small selection of cichlids from Lake Tanganyika has served as an acceptable introductory display of the spectacular diversity of species that inhabit one of the most amazing lakes on earth. To have covered every known species and color variant would require a book of several hundred pages in length. I encourage those of you with a love of animals and, in particular, a love of cichlids to delve further into this fascinating group from Africa's oldest lake. Enjoy!

This new cichlid species was collected in deep water at Chituta Bay, Zambia, as a by-catch of Xenotilapia sp. *"Fluorescent Green." Only further scientific analysis will determine if it belongs to a known genus or if a new genus will need to be created for it.*

GLOSSARY

Anoxic: totally devoid of oxygen

Bicuspid: teeth having two pointed projections at the end

Biotope: a living organism's natural habitat

Brood parasitism: Form of reproduction in catfish, particularly *Synodontis multipunctatus,* in which the catfish adds to the eggs in the mouth of a mouthbrooding cichlid. After the catfish eggs hatch, the young devour the cichlid embryos, a first food source.

Carnivore: flesh-eating animal

Conspecifics: term applied to individuals of the same species

Cryptic: camouflage; an animal with a color pattern that mimics the color or shape of its habitat

Ctenoid scale: circular scale with several small pointed projections on its outer edge

Cycloid scale: circular scale with smooth edges all around

Dither fish: any species of fish incidental to the primary aquarium residents

Herbivorous: plant-eating animal

Heterotrophic bacteria: bacteria that are capable of using various organic materials for their food and energy needs

kH: carbonate hardness; the measurement of the amount of carbonate or bicarbonate in water

Lateral line: A series of receptors embedded in the scales of a fish that can usually be seen as a narrow line running horizontally down the body. These receptors enable the fish to detect movement in the water nearby.

Lyrate: suggesting the shape of a lyre, as a fish tail

Mollusks: shelled invertebrates, such as snails and clams

Pelagic: living in the open water away from the shoreline

pH: A value on a scale of 0 to 14 that indicates the acidity or alkalinity of water. Acidic water is less than 7, neutral water is 7, and alkaline water is higher than 7.

Pharyngeal bones: bones in the throat and studded with teeth that aid in the mastication of food

Phytoplankton: microscopic plants, usually algae, that float in the water

Piscivore, piscivorous: an animal that eats fish

Planktivorous: an animal that eats free-floating phytoplankton and zooplankton

Polyphyletic: a group of related organisms derived from several distinct ancestors

Tribe: a taxonomic category that consists of several closely related genera

Tricuspid: tooth having three pointed projections at the end

Zooplankton: tiny aquatic animals, usually crustacean and insect larvae, that float in the water

Neolamprologus sexfasciatus male from Kipili, Tanzania.

INFORMATION

Magazines

Tropical Fish Hobbyist
TFH Publications, Inc.
211 West Sylvania Avenue
Neptune, NJ 07753
(908)-988-8400

Aquarium Fish
Fancy Publications, Inc.
Subscription Department
P.O. Box 53351
Boulder, CO 80323-3351

Cichlid News
Aquatic Promotions, Inc.
P.O. Box 522842
Miami, FL 33152
(305)-593-0088

Journals

Ichthyological Exploration of Fresh Waters
Verlag Dr. Friedrich Pfeil
P.O. Box 65 00 86
D-81214, Munchen, Germany

Books

Brichard, Pierre. *Book of Cichlids and All the Fishes of Lake Tanganyika.* Neptune, NJ: TFH Publications, 1989.
Konings, Ad and Horst Walter Diekhoff. *Tanganyika Secrets.* St. Leon-Rot, Germany: Cichlid Press, 1992.
Konings, Ad. *Enjoying Cichlids.* St. Leon-Rot, Germany, Cichlid Press, 1993.
____. *Back to Nature Guide to Tanganyika Cichlids.* 2nd Edition. El Paso, TX, Cichlid Press, 2005.
____. *Tanganyika Cichlids in their natural habitat.* El Paso, TX, Cichlid Press, 1998.

National Cichlid Clubs

American Cichlid Association
524 Prairie Knoll Drive
Naperville, IL 60565

Pacific Coast Cichlid Association
P.O. Box 28145
San Jose, CA 95128

Greater Chicago Cichlid Association
41 West 510 Route 20
Hampshire, IL 60140

International Cichlid Clubs

England
British Cichlid Association
248 Longridge, Knutsford
Cheshire, WA18 8PH

France
Association France Cichlid
15 Rue des Hirondelles
F-67350 Daunendorf

Germany
Deutsche Cichliden Gesellschaft
Parkstraße 21a
D-33719 Bielfeld

Netherlands
Nederlandse Cichliden Vereniging
Boeier 31
NL-1625 CJ Hoorn

Important Note

Electrical equipment for aquarium care is described in this book. Please do not fail to read the note below, because serious accidents could occur if you do not do so.

Water damage from broken glass, overflows, or tank leaks cannot always be avoided; therefore, you should have insurance against accidents.

Please take special care that neither children nor adults ever eat any aquarium plants. They can cause serious health problems. Fish medication should be kept away from children.

Safety Around the Aquarium

Water and electricity can lead to dangerous accidents; therefore, you should make absolutely certain when buying equipment that it is suitable for use in an aquarium.

Every mechanical device must have the UL sticker on it. These letters assure that the safety of the equipment has been carefully checked by experts and that, with ordinary use, nothing dangerous can happen.

Always unplug any electrical equipment before you do any cleaning around or in the aquarium.

Never do your own repairs on the aquarium or its equipment if something is wrong with either of them. All repairs should be done only by an expert.

Dedication

To Marmie, co-heir in Christ and my devoted soul mate

About the Author

Mark Phillip Smith is a professional wildlife photographer, explorer, and discoverer of freshwater temperate and tropical fishes. He contributed to the discovery of a new genus and two species of Lake Malawi cichlids in 1990 and, more recently, to the discovery of a new Lamprologus species in the Lower Congo. In 1994, he discovered several new species of cichlids in Lake Edward, Uganda. His ichthyological interests have taken him to the Philippines, Mexico, Uruguay, Malawi, Zambia, Zimbabwe, Kenya, Uganda, England, Sweden, Japan, Hawaii, and the Caribbean. He writes for, and provides photographs to, domestic and international publications, and is the author of three books on cichlids for Barron's.

Acknowledgments

The author wishes to thank the following people who over the years offered their hospitality and permission to photograph their fish. Many have given of their time to help me understand various perplexing concepts and ideas, and some have contributed outstanding photographs. Thanks to them for their patience with my seemingly endless bombardment of questions, theories, and ideas. My deepest apologies if I have inadvertently omitted anyone who figured significantly in my evolving knowledge of the cichlids of Lake Tanganyika.

Thomas Anderson, Dr. George Barlow, Rich and Laura Birley, Pat Brokaw, Dr. Warren Burgess, Ron Coleman, Doug Conkling, Laif Demason, Phil Farrel, Lee Finley of Finley Aquatic Books, Kjell Fohrman, Jim and Agnus Forshey, Tim Hovanec, Ray Hunziker, Aaron Kerrigan of Kerrigan's Aquatics, Dr. Ad Konings, Rene Kruter, Dr. Paul Loiselle, John Lombardo, Steve Lundblad, Bill Nelson, Rob Nelsen, John Niemans, Art North, Ralph Paccione, Michel and Clotilde Perbost, Chuck Rambo, Robert Rodriquez, Ben Rosler, Peter Rubin of Atlantis Tropical Fish, Harold Scheel, Delores Schehr, Dr. Robert Schelly of the American Museum of Natural History, David Schleser, Ron Sousy, Chip Spiegel of Blue Chip Aquatics, Dr. Melanie Stiassny, Dick Strever, Stan Sung, Jerry Walls, and Kurt Zadnick.

Cover Photos

Mark Smith

Photo Credits

Thomas Anderson: pp. 88 (top and bottom) and 91 (bottom) and Ad Konings: pp. 7 (top and bottom), 44 (top), 45 (top right and bottom), 46 (top), 50 (bottom), 51 (top left), 60 (top left), 63 (top right), 66 (bottom), 68 (bottom), 79 (top), 81 (bottom), 85 (top left), and 86 (top). All other photos by Mark Smith.

Thumbnail Photo Species

Chapter 1: *Altolamprologus compressiceps* Chaitika; Chapter 2: *Neolamprologus buescheri* Gombi; Chapter 3: *Neolamprologus pulcher*; Chapter 4: *Neolamprologus leleupi*; and Chapter 5: *Altolamprologus calvus*.

© Copyright 2008, 1998 by Barron's Educational Series, Inc.

All inquiries should be addressed to:
Barron's Educational Series, Inc.
250 Wireless Boulevard
Hauppauge, NY 11788
www.barronseduc.com

Library of Congress Catalog Card No. 2007011554

ISBN-13: 978-0-7641-3673-3
ISBN-10: 0-7641-3673-9

Library of Congress Cataloging-in-Publication Data
Smith, Mark Phillip, 1966–
    Lake Tanganyika cichlids : everything about history, setting up an aquarium, health concerns, and spawning / Mark Phillip Smith ; full-color photographs ; illustrations by Michele Earle-Bridges.
        p. cm.
    Includes bibliographical references and index.
    ISBN-13: 978-0-7641-3673-3 (alk. paper)
    ISBN-10: 0-7641-3673-9 (alk. paper)
    1. Cichlids—Tanganyika, Lake. 2. Aquarium fishes.
I. Title.

SF458.C5S544   2008
639.3'774—dc22   2007011554

Printed in China
9 8 7 6 5 4 3 2 1